TERENCE CONRAN

A SORT OF AUTOBIOGRAPHY

HarperCollins*Publishers*

Worried about life in a Cone chair, 1954.

Enjoying life (and a cigar) in a Karuselli chair, 2001.

To my many friends and relations who have supported the wobbly ladders throughout my life.

As W R Lethaby wrote, 'For the earlier part of my life I was quieted by being told that ours was the richest country in the world until I woke up to know that what I meant by riches was learning and beauty, music and art, coffee and omelette: perhaps in the coming days of poverty, we may get more of these.'

I agree, but I would only add a cigar and a glass of wine now and again.

Terence Conran.

COMMISSIONING EDITOR: Richard Atkinson
CONTRIBUTING EDITOR: Elizabeth Wilhide
ART DIRECTOR: Helen Lewis
PICTURE RESEARCHER: Clare Limpus

Colour origination by Colourscan, Singapore
Printed and bound by Editoriale Johnson, Italy

AUTHOR'S ACKNOWLEDGEMENT
My particular thanks to Liz Wilhide, who acted as my editorial Mother Superior and in Richard Atkinson's words, 'did her best to save me from myself'; Clare Limpus, who researched the pictures and discovered images that jogged my memory with things I had long since forgotten; Helen Lewis, who, as always, has art-directed the book with graphic style and helped to make it, I hope, a new sort of autobiography; and Sam Newman, who typed, corrected and typed again and again the answers.

First published in 2001 by
HarperCollins*Publishers*
77–85 Fulham Palace Road
London W6 8JB

The HarperCollins website address is: www.**fire**and**water**.com

A CIP catalogue record for this book is available from the British Library.

ISBN: 0 00 711529 6
05 04 03 02 01
9 8 7 6 5 4 3 2 1

CONTENTS

FOREWORD

A SORT OF AUTOBIOGRAPHY

You once told a journalist that writing an autobiography is 'egotism on wheels'. How do you justify this book?

NICHOLAS IND

You are right; I despise autobiographies, and biographies written while the subject is alive – as my biographer you will have been all too aware of my reluctance in this respect! But the question-and-answer format of this book seems to be a version of 'egotism on wheels' that I can live with, since I shall not be able to answer questions from the grave and since it has given anyone who was interested the chance to ask me virtually anything.

I hope it will prove a rather more interesting read than the standard autobiography that tends to filter out bits that the autobiographer chooses to forget. Rereading my answers I realize that I sound opinionated, naive at times, disagreeable, even arrogant, which perhaps I am! At any rate, I have enjoyed doing it, egotism or not, even if at times the process has been somewhat akin to lying on a psychiatrist's couch and even if it has meant exposing quite a few warts. It's been a cathartic, stimulating experience.

The invitation to write this book came from Richard Atkinson at HarperCollins; it is meant to be a celebration of my seventieth birthday. Inevitably, this has made me think about getting old. More and more I realize that I try to persuade myself that my mind is not fossilizing and that the ideas still flow, that my talents are not diminished even if my body is. I also try to believe that all my experience and knowledge must contribute to making my work more mature and thoughtful than the efforts of all those young pretenders. Sadly, this is only partially true. Freshness and naivety are recognizably very attractive qualities and present a strong challenge to the seen-that, done-that cynicism of the older creative person. But I also like to think of the many painters, sculptors, designers, writers and architects who have kept going well past retirement age, some of whom have even done their best work at my time of life. I hope it will be the same for me.

When we were putting together this book, we invited members of the public to submit questions via e-mail or postcards, an invitation publicized in a variety of locations, from the Design Museum to our magazine *Live It*. But a large proportion of the questions featured in this 'sort of' autobiography have come from friends, family, colleagues and acquaintances who were specifically requested to participate. Many came up with multiple questions, which related to different periods of my life or aspects of my career. Inevitably, many also asked very similar questions – a disconcertingly large number of these questions seemed to concern how, when, or whether I was ever going to retire! To provide some coherence for the reader and preserve an element of narrative flow, questions and their answers have been loosely grouped both chronologically and thematically, which means that the same questioner may pop up at different places in the book.

At the same time, not everyone responded or accepted; one of the most graceful refusals came from David Dimbleby, who noted that the format of Q & A did not 'permit supplementary questions' – anathema, I suppose, for such a seasoned interviewer and journalist. It's true Q & A is not fully interactive – that would truly be a lifetime's work – but I hope it provides an unusual departure from what is more normally a wholly one-sided tale.

I have tried to answer at least one question from each of the contributors (some of whom sent in a dozen or more) but finally, after much persuasion on the part of my editor, I have reluctantly agreed to omit Jonathan Meades' incredibly crude offering (and my reply to it). It's the only such omission in the book, but I'm happy to say that neither the question nor the answer sheds any particular light on my life and career. I have to agree that my editors are always right – I only wish that the people with whom I've worked over the years could have learned the same lesson about me. Jonathan, if you're *that* interested in senior Tory politicians, I can show you what I wrote next time we meet.

I knew when I was knee-high to a grasshopper that I was going to be a household name. You are a household name in more ways than one since you literally create households. When did the mosquito of ambition first pierce your epidermis? I want to read about your childhood ambitions, your early dreams, your teenage disappointments. I want to know when you first set your Hush Puppy on the lowest rung of the Habitat ladder to greatness.

Would it be simpler if I wrote this book for you?
DAME EDNA EVERAGE

Yes.

STEPHEN BAYLEY

Richard Atkinson
HarperCollins
77-85 Fulham Road
London
W6 8JB

25th October 2000

Dear Richard

Terence Conran

Thanks for yours of the 19th.

How hilarious and how typical that Terence should want to do an autobiography and expect other people to do the work !

Of course, I'm not unwilling to help, except that the only question I'd want to ask and the only answer worth hearing would probably not be ones you'd wish to print.

I'd suggest you publish this letter in facsimile, perhaps as endpapers. Alternatively, I could search my archives for the letter from Fatty that included the words "jumped-up", "little" and "prick" all in the opening sentence. It's a classic.

With best wishes,

On holiday at Studland Bay.

CHILDHOOD

I was born on 4 October 1931 in Esher, Surrey. Soon afterwards, we moved to London to a flat in Hampstead, where my sister Priscilla was born in 1936. I went to Arnold House School in Hampstead, then as a boarder to Boxgrove near Guildford until just before the outbreak of war when the whole family left London for Liphook in Hampshire.

Memories of my childhood are inextricably bound up with the war. I am most definitely a war child, brought up in an era of 'make do and mend', an era that lasted long after hostilities ceased; I wouldn't say that we suffered extreme privation, but there was a general sense of scarcity of practically everything, from food and heat to toys and books. The result was that both my sister and I were thrown onto our own resources from an early age. Leaving London to escape the Blitz meant that I spent my childhood in a very beautiful (although not entirely safe) part of the countryside, a setting that inspired my very first passions for native wild flowers, butterflies and moths.

What is your earliest memory?
STAFFORD CLIFF

Lying in my pram under apple blossom in my parents' garden in Esher, Surrey. And another memory that dates from soon after: spilling a can of bright green paint on the terracotta floor in the kitchen. The clash of colours was truly disgusting!

The following interview, with Priscilla and me, is a rather loose memoir of our childhood years.

Do you remember when Priscilla was born?

TERENCE:
I have this vague memory of her being born; it was when we lived in Canfield Gardens, Hampstead, just behind the department store John Barnes, and I remember my mother sort of lurching around the flat with this babe.

What sort of relationship did you have with your mother; was she a distant person when you were growing up?

PRISCILLA:
I think she probably was disorganized, and she was very bookish.

TERENCE:
She read and read and read like mad; always did the *Times* crossword in ten minutes or something like that.

PRISCILLA:
'Distant' is not the right word to describe her; I think she was perhaps a bit mystified by life. She'd had a horrible childhood; her mother died when she was six and her father when she

With Priscilla.

was twelve. She was brought up by old aunts who told her she was very ugly when she wasn't; then she was made to be a secretary so she could earn her living when really what she wanted to do was to go to art school.

TERENCE:
Both Priscilla and I absolutely get our creative talents through her, although our father used to draw a bit.

PRISCILLA:
He did wonderful pen and inks, quite tight but pretty competent.

TERENCE:
But our mother was the one with the eye, the one who took us to exhibitions and bought our toys at Heal's and things like that. I remember – because my father once upset a bottle of Indian ink on the floor – that our living room at Canfield Gardens had a rather plain beige carpet and big, white linen loose-covered blocky sofas and chairs. That simplicity was very much her taste.

PRISCILLA:
I guess our household was never particularly starchy. Up until the war my mother just had someone called a 'tweenie', which was a between-maid, somebody that did everything. Although our granny used to sweep into the nursery in scarlet chiffon and terrify the pants off everybody.

This grandmother, our father's mother, was the most extraordinary character. During the war you weren't allowed to go to Italy and she pretended to be Mussolini's mistress to get into the country. She did some outrageous things like that; she used to go out to Shanghai because it was the fashionable thing to do.

TERENCE:
She got stuck in Shanghai during the war and she had diabetes; I can always remember my father rushing round trying to get insulin to send out to her.

PRISCILLA:
She also decided to become a Catholic, which was terribly fashionable in the 1920s. She sent our father to a Jesuit school, where he was beaten every day for the good of his soul. When he married our mother he decided to come out of the Catholic Church for good.

Did you have a nanny?

TERENCE:

Yes, and she was a very important part of both of our lives. Her name was Jenny Envis but she wasn't Envis then, that was after she married the greenkeeper of Liphook Golf Club, a man called Bertie. She went off during the war and became a teleprinter operator in the Auxiliary Territorial Service. She was remarkable; although she been brought up in a very, very poor Welsh family, she was very intelligent.

PRISCILLA:

Our nanny had been one of six children. Her father had been a sailor and her mother had literally had to take in washing to bring them up. I knew her mother; she was a very modest lady but I think she had quite a will, because she would have needed one to have brought all that lot up by herself.

Jenny was originally put into service, as they say, with the Duke of Westminster. That's where she trained to be a nanny, working alongside some awful old battle-axe. But she was clearly very bright and she became a very good friend to our mother, who liked reading a lot; Jenny used to read alongside and then they discussed the books together.

What sort of influence did your nanny have on you? Was she very strict?

TERENCE:

Not at all. I remember she took me off to Felpham, near Bognor Regis, on seaside holidays with other nannies, and it was on one of those holidays that I got into an argument with von Ribbentrop's son and hit him on the head with a metal spade. I always claim that I started the Second World War!

PRISCILLA:

I think our nanny loved us; it was so clear that she loved us and it was an uncomplicated love, I suspect. She was very supportive to us both.

TERENCE:

Absolutely, we were her children.

What was your father like?

TERENCE:
My father had a rather brutal upbringing. I don't think his mother took any interest in him at all.

PRISCILLA:
His father – Bertie – didn't pay him much attention either, just dropped him a gold sovereign every time he saw him, which wasn't very often. I think he was probably a very, very lonely person.

TERENCE:
But he was a very good-looking man – apparently all the old gays fancied him like mad. He was also quite a sporty fellow; he played rugby for Rosslyn Park, that was his real passion. And he had an Amilcar that broke its back axle on Westminster Bridge; one of its wheels, I remember him telling me, rolled off and went right over the edge into the Thames.

PRISCILLA:
Our father was this funny sort of mixture, very Irish in a way, a mixture of deep sentiment and a kind of violence.

TERENCE:
When he'd had too much to drink, which was fairly frequently, his character changed totally, and he went from being a really nice, charming, cheerful, sweet man to being just awful. He was a fairly bitter person.

PRISCILLA:
Bitter that the world had done him out of what he should have had, which I think in some ways was true. I don't know how much pleasure we gave him. We were both fairly secure as children and fairly forthright, as we probably are now, and I think we made someone as insecure as he was feel rather uncomfortable. Don't you think?

TERENCE:
I don't know. I saw a lot of him before he died, when he went into a nursing home near Barton Court and his old family home West Woodhay, and he was always extremely proud of what we'd achieved. I think he was very sad; he obviously loved our mother very deeply and when she died relatively young at sixty-two he felt completely lost. He was very sentimental.

LEFT: *The wedding day of my parents, Rupert Conran and Christina Halstead, in 1928.*

ABOVE: *My parents went abroad together only once in their lives, for their honeymoon in St Maxim, in the south of France. I've no idea who the woman on the right is – but presumably she was attached to whoever was taking the picture!*

RIGHT: *Me as a baby sitting on my mother's lap.*

Were you frightened of him?

PRISCILLA:
Yes.

TERENCE:
When he was drunk, yes; only when he was drunk.

PRISCILLA:
I think he was actually quite violent with you, he wasn't with me but he was with you. That used to outrage me; I used to go and bite him, actually. He used to try to smack you and I used to run along after him.

TERENCE:
You know, I've completely blotted that out of my memory. I just remember hating the fact that when he'd drunk half a bottle of whisky he changed into somebody who was so brutal. How our mother stood it, I'll never know, but she managed to get through all right.

PRISCILLA:
I don't know whether she did or whether that was one of the reasons that she had cancer.

TERENCE:
I saw quite a lot of them when I had a cottage up in Dalham near my factory at Thetford and they used to come up and stay there. If she could keep him off the booze he was fine.

What did your father do for a living?

TERENCE:
First of all he worked in the Rubber Exchange and then he formed this business called Conran and Company Limited, which he later gave to me when I first started up. The business operated on the Thames, importing gum copal, which was used to make paints and varnishes. Gum copal, gum tragacanth, gum arabic and also crepe rubber.

PRISCILLA:
He used to bring bits home. And that's why he didn't go to the war, because one of the things he was doing was processing rubber, which was considered essential to the war effort.

TERENCE:

The business was down in Stepney, between Tower Bridge and Canary Wharf on the other side of the river from Butlers Wharf. It was bombed during the raids on London and there was a huge fire that melted all the resin so that it literally flowed down the nearby streets. Most of the equipment was destroyed, practically everything except the safe, which, when it was recovered, was found to be totally encased in resin. I have a vivid memory of chipping away at the safe like a huge bar of toffee. But the business was completely wiped out; afterwards my father went to work as a representative for a paint company.

PRISCILLA:

Our parents really didn't have a lot of fun, because quite soon after they had married and had us they were straight into the war.

TERENCE:

The only time they ever went abroad together was for their honeymoon, to St Maxim in the south of France. They were very broke as well; they had virtually no money. Both sets of my grandparents had lost all their money in the stock market crash of the 1920s so my father, who had been quite well off up till then and had never needed to work seriously for his living, had to find a proper job to make money. We used to get sent a chicken every week, which was a great luxury, by our great-grandmother.

PRISCILLA:

Great-granny was an extraordinary lady. She wore black bombazine and her shoes had little rubber heels – she used to do her own shoe mending, even though she was quite rich.

TERENCE:

She chewed every mouthful ninety-nine times; she had a very, very powerful lavender scent and she used to drive my mother absolutely mad. A real Victorian.

How did the loss of the family money affect you? Growing up, were you aware of it?

TERENCE:

You just knew. Like typical middle-class parents, my father worked and worked away to pay for our education and we both went to quite good schools.

PRISCILLA:

I used to go up the Burlington Arcade with our mother and a suitcase full of family silver – usually before the term began – to flog it off. It was Cromwellian silver.

Before the war I went to Arnold House School in Hampstead.

TERENCE:

We also had some wonderful Dutch flower pictures that were sold. All the beautiful things that our parents had inherited were gradually sold off to pay the school fees.

PRISCILLA:

I remember at one point our mother having to give up her *Times*, which was very precious to her. But I don't think it had the reaction that you would have expected, that we would work extra hard and be frightfully diligent. I actually think that it made me feel a bit bloody-minded. Personally I felt that them giving everything up for us was too much of a weight.

TERENCE:

I remember being very concerned and worrying about how broke they were. I remember my father once losing a ten-shilling note and looking everywhere for it. He was really distressed he'd lost it. He'd spent it in the pub, I expect.

Were you evacuated from London during the war?

PRISCILLA:

Just before war broke out we left Canfield Gardens. I know the building was bombed and the roof came off, so it was just as well that we escaped when we did. Then we went to our Auntie Tom's, which was the family house in Midhurst, and all I remember about it is that it was very gloomy.

TERENCE:

I remember my parents talking about 'the war' at least a year before it happened. I was sent away to a school at Boxgrove as a boarder; Alexander Plunket Greene, who later married Mary Quant, was there as well. We then moved to this house in Liphook in Hampshire, Old Shepherd's Farm.

The Germans soon discovered that there was a huge arms dump in Liphook and came and bombed it, and there were lots of air battles. My father joined the Home Guard. Then I went to Highfield school as a day-boy, which was a walk across the fields. It was a very High Church prep school for Eton.

PRISCILLA:

There you met Chenevix-Trench, who encouraged your interest in biology.

TERENCE:

Yes, you're absolutely right, I was always passionate about collecting butterflies and moths and wild flowers; there was a great moment when I managed to catch a silver-striped hawk moth. The other thing I remember about Highfield was winning the 'Jacks' competition; they used to have these competitions to design posters and I won with a drawing of a monster. I was absolutely thrilled.

Did you find the war frightening?

PRISCILLA:

I think there was a bit of fright, because our parents were very frightened. We had something we called the black hole of Calcutta, a little bolt-hole that must have had a small stove in it at one time because it had very solid walls. There was a black table in the hole and we used to creep underneath this table during raids.

TERENCE:

There was a lot of bombing around the area. I remember one night they'd failed to hit the arms dump and they thought, right, we're going to saturate the whole area with incendiary bombs. The haystacks caught light at the farm next door, and the Germans must have thought they'd got the dump, so they dive-bombed the farm.

PRISCILLA:

The farm had an open vat of petrol that they'd hoarded for their tractors and the Home Guard had to push this open vat out of the way or there would have been the most almighty explosion. The next morning all the mushrooms came up.

TERENCE:

The fields were absolutely white with mushrooms because the heat from incendiary bombs had warmed the ground.

PRISCILLA;

We really were living on a farm then. They had a dairy, they had pigs, carthorses . . .

TERENCE:

. . . Land girls.

PRISCILLA:

You *would* remember the land girls, I remember the carthorses. It was quite tough for our mother, because she had to do everything. It was very, very cold. We had a bathroom that you really dreaded entering and we used to have bowl baths.

TERENCE:

There was no form of central heating and only very small fireplaces that gave out practically no heat at all.

PRISCILLA:

On the mantelpiece we had 'Sunday toys', which were wonderful things that our mother's father had brought back from all over the world. There were cherrystone slippers that came from Russia, a little hare made of ivory that came from China.

TERENCE:

Beautiful little things. My grandfather used to collect snuffboxes as well; his collection of them was given to the V & A.

PRISCILLA:

On Sundays the toys were brought down very carefully for us to look at. We had a huge advantage in not having a lot of things. All children have imaginations and this probably encouraged us to use and develop ours.

TERENCE:

My mother was very encouraging, finding the space where I could set up a workshop and letting me build a wood-fired pottery kiln in the garden. I remember the first firing, opening the kiln after it had cooled down and being thrilled to discover that practically all the pots had survived. Priscilla was mad about horses and she was given riding lessons.

A family group. My parents, Priscilla and I, photographed in the garden of Old Shepherd's Farm during the war.

PRISCILLA:
And I had rabbits. We had nasty geese that used to peck our legs.

TERENCE:
We had a pig once as well, a pig for the pot. I think it was a passing fancy to try and eke out our rations.

PRISCILLA:
We were much better fed than city children because we had a garden and grew an awful lot of our own food. With our dad being in the Home Guard, there was definitely trading going on, a healthy black market. I think deer were shot that ought not to have been.

TERENCE:
Across the other side of the road, there was what had been an extraordinary garden, Chiltley Park, which had become completely wild. It had a walled garden and all sorts of

The male Common Blue butterfly (Polyommatus icarus); the female is brown. As a child, I was always passionate about collecting moths, butterflies and wild flowers.

RIGHT: *The sort of natural habitat, full of wild flowers, that is a perfect breeding ground for butterflies and moths but is sadly fast disappearing from our countryside.*

things grew there, including peaches and loganberries, which I used to go across and collect. The place was utterly abandoned. But I spent a lot of my time at boarding school and there the food was *dire*, even after the war was over. The boys at Bryanston thought the cook was selling our ration coupons. We were always hungry.

What are the first things you remember making?

TERENCE:
I think it was a bookcase. I was about ten years old and my mother had to persuade me rather forcibly to finish it properly.

PRISCILLA:
During the war we went to visit our Aunt Doff [Dorothy Knowling] at Cornwood in Devon. While we were there I remember Terence made a little boat he called 'Mousey'. He used to make the boats solid and then groove them out in the middle, cut them and restick them together so they were planked. And this one had jam cupboards in the cabin, which endeared me to it, tiny little cupboards with small pots of jam and a little brass anchor. We used to sail Mousey in the little ponds at the bottom of the garden where there was a bubbling stream. The front garden path of Aunt Doff's cottage had alpine strawberries down the side, which is why I grow them at my cottage garden as a memory of her.

TERENCE:
And is no doubt why I have them in my front garden, too! Up on the moor there were huge ferns growing in all the trees and there were sundew fly-catchers and sphagnum moss.

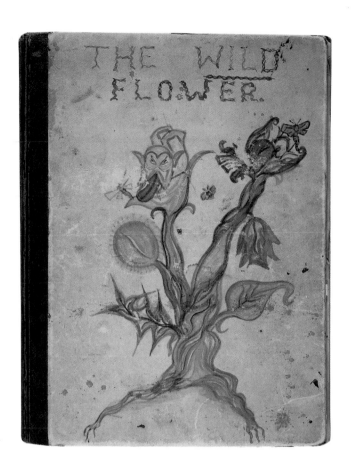

I was terribly proud of my pressed wild flower book, which my Aunt Doff encouraged me to make. I painted a fly-catching monster on the cover.

38 Plume Spear Thistle and leaves.
This is very common and is the thistle that one everyone sees. Flowering from July to October.

39 Musk Thistle and leaves.
Not very common, but may be found on moorland or in some sheltered hollow of the south downs. It flowers from June to the end of September.

40 White burdock and leaves
This is a variation from the common Burdock with the red flower. It grows in the same places as the ordinary burdock but far less frequently. Flowering from June to September

38

39

Plume-
spear thistle
and leaves

40.

Musk Thistle
and leaves

White burdock and leaves

16

PRISCILLA:

And that was where you made your first pressed flower book. Aunt Doff was very interested in flowers and gardens. She was a personal friend of the Dalai Lama – she used to go out to Tibet and find wonderful plants and take them back to Scotland where somebody she knew had a big garden.

TERENCE:

This visit would have been when I was about eleven. I started making things to sell about a year later when I had appendicitis which became peritonitis and I was off school for six months recuperating in a sanatorium. That was between leaving Highfield and going to Bryanston. Because I was so bored one of the doctors encouraged me to make things and I made doll's house furniture and other toys that my mother took down to the local toy shop and offered them on a sale-or-return basis.

PRISCILLA:

Rabbit roundabouts. They had a dowel that went in the top and twizzled around and matchboxes with little scenes painted inside. And you made very small cricket bats, which you used to make properly, with rubber down the shaft. Very small.

TERENCE:

I made a battleship model, of HMS *Hood* or something like that, which I swapped. I think my father must have greased the palm of the local publican at Liphook; he had been a railway engineer and he had a wonderful workshop. In the garden of the pub, which was called the Royal Anchor Hotel, he had a model railway that you could actually sit on. I swapped this battleship model that I'd made for a 3½-inch Myford lathe, which was absolutely my pride and joy.

PRISCILLA:

And then you went and got a piece of metal in your eye.

TERENCE:

I was turning metal in the lathe and a bit flew out and stuck in my left pupil; ever since, all I have been able to see out of that eye is just pale shapes and blobs of colour. The accident did get me out of National Service later on and thus saved two or three years of my life, which seems a fair exchange; as far as I was concerned at the time the main difference was that I used to play cricket left-handed and then I had to change to playing right-handed.

You are both passionate about good food. Was this one of your parents' interests?

PRISCILLA:

When my mother was a child growing up in Chichester, she wasn't allowed to be in the kitchen. It wasn't considered quite nice to be there, but she adored the cook, Old Ede, who used to sneak her glasses of lemonade and things like that.

TERENCE:

I remember my mother telling me that Old Ede used to have a large bun on the top of her head and she kept a lizard in her bun as a pet. Apparently some butcher's boy came to deliver the meat and when the cook opened the door he fainted!

PRISCILLA:

When our mother met our father she couldn't even boil an egg, so our father taught her and then she went on to be really quite interested in cooking. She would cook all week for a dinner party. Our parents were quite unusual in that they appreciated good food. I seem to remember our father bringing home a bottle of wine every now and again, sitting us down and saying, what do you think of that, and discussing it, which must have been very rare.

TERENCE:

Very few people drank wine with their meals in those days. One of our father's great friends was a man called Ronnie Driver, who had quite a lot of money. He and my father used to go out to black market restaurants in Soho in the late 1940s, early '50s. For Christmas Ronnie always used to send my mother a pot of that terrible so-called foie gras from Fortnum & Mason and also a pot of caviar. I don't know whether my mother was a good cook, but she was certainly very interested. It was quite difficult during the war years to be a good cook.

PRISCILLA:

I remember that on top of the stove she always used to have a great pot of handkerchiefs boiling away beside the curry; that's a definite vision of childhood.

TERENCE:

One of the worst things that ever happened to me was much later when I was a student and I had come back home one evening; I was standing by the stove with her and she was frying something and I pulled out my handkerchief, sneezed and a condom came out and fell into the frying pan. She laughed like mad, I can remember. I was so embarrassed.

You've worked together in the past. Do you think that your shared outlook comes from your childhood?

PRISCILLA:

What our mother passed on to us was that if you had an ability it was your duty to take it as far as you possibly could. We were given a very, very strong work ethic; I can't think otherwise why we would both like working so much.

TERENCE:

We also have an extraordinarily similar eye. I always remember this time when we were on a buying trip in India together turning over this huge pile of carpets and we both chose the same twenty-seven carpets.

PRISCILLA:

It was quite a shock, that, actually, because it was the first time in our adult life that we realized there was this strong link.

TERENCE:

I've always felt that if my mother had lived in this age, she'd have been doing very much the same sort of thing as Priscilla and I are doing now.

With Priscilla in India. Fabindia in Delhi was a major supplier of fabric to Habitat. John Bissell, who was married to Bim (next to me, in the sari), ran the company; they became close friends of ours.

A cast tabletop that I made. Note the Paolozzi influence.

EDUCATION

After Highfield, my prep school, I went to Bryanston in Blandford, Dorset, arriving there at the beginning of 1945 and leaving a few years later when I was sixteen to study textile design at the Central School of Arts and Crafts in London. At Bryanston I gained a few School Certificates, but a great deal more besides; and Central really opened my eyes and introduced me to exciting new ideas about art and design. But, like many people, I was perhaps even more influenced by what you might call my 'informal' education, the formative experiences I had when I was young and the people who were around me.

Connaught House, Bryanston, 1947.

What sort of a vision did you gain from Thorold Coade, Don Potter and other masters? Was this reflected in your attitude to work?

JOHN ROSE

I arrived at Bryanston after a long period convalescing from peritonitis. The school was my mother's choice and it was an inspired one; most of the boys who had been at my prep school, Highfield, went on to Eton and other more conventionally academic schools. My mother had always encouraged what she saw as a creative and entrepreneurial spark in me and thought that Bryanston would develop these talents; it turned out to be a very important decision.

Having come from a very traditional prep school, I particularly enjoyed the general air of modernity and creativity. I found the Dalton educational philosophy that Bryanston had adopted very much to my taste. This rather unconventional system meant that each of us was assigned an individual tutor who oversaw our progress on a regular basis. We all had charts that set out our different lessons and these were marked by each master. The tutor, who acted almost as a personal 'headmaster', would then review and discuss the results with us at the end of each week.

Unfortunately, my tutor died during my last year at the school; more fortunately, for me at least, the school neglected to replace him. This meant that there was no one to check whether or not I had been in Latin in any particular week, which was just as well since I was generally down in the pottery instead. I had a fantastic time.

As headmaster, Coade was very much a 'higher being' and his presence was much respected. But the two masters who made the greatest impression upon me were Charles Handley-Read, who taught art and would not have been at Bryanston at all except for the fact that he had been a conscientious objector during the war, and Don Potter, who taught pottery, metalwork and sculpture. Although my mother was interested in art and design, I didn't really focus on it until I was at Bryanston and had the benefit of their teaching.

Don Potter, with his obvious enthusiasms for earthly pleasures, enthusiasms that he disseminated so brilliantly, was a perfect contrast to Coade. He himself had been taught to carve and sculpt by Eric Gill and was also very influenced by Bernard Leach, influences that I absorbed in turn.

One of the aspects of life at Bryanston that I found very character-forming was 'pioneering'. Sadly, this part of the curriculum has now been abandoned; in fact, I keep urging the school to bring it back. Pioneering, which took place on three of the six afternoons when one would normally have had games, involved all kinds of practical, physical activities, everything from digging the vegetable garden to learning the rudiments of plumbing. I learned how to lay bricks and helped to build a boathouse and an observatory, among other projects. We also made school visits to nearby country houses, such as Montacute, and I can remember feeling an instant affinity with the kitchens and dairies 'below stairs' as opposed to the grand state rooms full of ornate furnishings. I also associate one of my earliest personal triumphs with Bryanston – catching a twenty-seven-pound pike all by myself from the River Stour! Unfortunately, it was quite disgusting when cooked.

Two covers of Saga, the Bryanston school magazine, both by me. I did the first as a student, just before I left, and the other as an old boy in 1997.

BRYANSTON SAGA

SPRING 1948

THE ON-GOING SAGA SUMMER 97

Bryanston, with its setting in the Dorset countryside, enabled me to pursue and develop my interests in butterflies, moths, beetles and wild flowers. And it was not too far away from the girls at Crichel House, as I soon discovered. I have had good reason to be grateful for the fact that Bryanston both understood my academic shortcomings and encouraged my talents. In today's climate, where exam results are of such concern, I'm not sure if I could have received such a sensitive and tailor-made education.

When did you first become aware of sex?

ALICE RAWSTHORN

There were plenty of opportunities to meet girls when I was at school; Cranborne Chase, the girls' school at Crichel House, was a bike ride away and it was in many ways the 'sister' school to Bryanston. But teenage frustrations were frequent. Not many girls believed in premarital sex and those who did I wasn't interested in anyway.

At the very end of my time at Bryanston I got caught out after making an assignation with a girl after hours. Coade, my headmaster, and Betty Galton, the headmistress of

Cranborne Chase, had some sort of conversation about it, as it seemed that the news had got round both schools. I wasn't exactly expelled – there were only a few days of term remaining – but Coade made it clear that it would be best if I left early. His argument was that if it appeared that he had done nothing about it, everyone else would think they could do the same and go off in the middle of the night on their bikes. I'm not saying who the girl was, but her brother later became a cabinet minister.

What influence did Dora Batty have on your life?

SHIRLEY CONRAN

Dora Batty, who was the head of the textile department at Central, saw quite quickly that my talent was for a whole range of design activities and encouraged me to take a job that wouldn't pigeonhole me. When I first arrived at Central to be interviewed by her, I had no idea what to bring. I took along my entire portfolio, which included a bit of everything that I had done up till then – from nature drawings to pressed flowers – so perhaps it wasn't entirely surprising that she gained this impression!

Before opting for textile design, I had discussed the options with my parents and my tutor at Bryanston. Because I had interests in organic chemistry, colour and pattern-making, all three came together to suggest a course in textile design and printing as further education. As it happened, and as Dora Batty was quick to grasp, during my textile course I found that I was even more interested in furniture design. It seems to me that the foundation year at design school is an ideal way of allowing students to experiment with different disciplines and it is surprising just how many change direction during this year, rather like I did.

Dora Batty was quite a strict teacher and you were expected to show up to classes and work hard, a discipline that was not much in evidence when I taught at the Royal College of Art twenty-five years ago; the students hardly ever bothered to turn up, achieving very little as a consequence. She ran the textile department brilliantly and brought in a whole raft of inspirational young designers and technicians as outside lecturers who really broadened our horizons. I learned how to screenprint but at the same time I absorbed the belief, which came from the Bauhaus and Arts and Crafts ideals that were much in evidence at Central, that good design should be something that was available to the whole community, not just to a few.

Ideals were practically all we had in those days. Out of my textile class at Central – there were thirty-three of us, mostly women – hardly anyone went on to get a job that was in any way related to what we were learning. Opportunities for design work were very rare. So perhaps Dora Batty's greatest influence on my life was to encourage me to take a job that I had been offered by the architect Denis Lennon instead of staying on at college to complete my degree.

When did you first become aware of modernist design? And what was your perception of it?

ALICE RAWSTHORN

I think I first understood the importance of modernism when I was a student in the late 1940s. The teachings of the Bauhaus and what it stood for had a major influence on me, as did the work of Le Corbusier. Later, in the 1950s, I went to the wonderful Triennales in Milan and was able to see first-hand the best of contemporary Italian design at a time when Italian designers were conquering the world.

At Central, when I was a student, many of the teachers modelled their courses on Bauhaus methods of design instruction and some had even studied under former Bauhaus teachers and artists such as Paul Klee. Before I went to Central, I had been heavily influenced by the Arts and Crafts movement, which emphasized the importance of craftwork and the role of design in improving life not merely for a few, but for everyone: I call it my 'William Morris' period. At Central I realized for the first time that mass production could be used in the same way and that industry had the potential to bring intelligent design to a wider audience, not least because prices could be kept at an affordable level. The trouble with one-off craft pieces is that they are often rather expensive, which keeps them out of the reach of the mainstream, as Morris discovered.

In the postwar period, when there was so much rebuilding to be done, modernism seemed to open up a new way of doing things and offer a chance to reshape the world in an exciting way. It also fitted perfectly with the democratic spirit of the times; people felt that they didn't want to go back to the old elitism. We felt that we were in the perfect position to put the Bauhaus ideals into practice, but in many ways we underestimated the conservatism of the 'powers that be'; it has taken a good half-century for Britain to begin to accept modernity.

What was the most rebellious thing you did as a student? Have you ever taken part in a demonstration?

REBECCA OATES

Sadly, the late 1940s and early '50s were not rebellious times. No parties, very little drink except cider, no drugs, no money and not much fun. Like many young people in the 1950s, I took part in CND marches and anti-Suez demonstrations. I really admired Aneurin Bevan, but I cannot say I was particularly active in a political sense.

I would love to hear who were your mentors in your youth. What sort of things did they help you appreciate? The ones I would most like to know about are the ones you actually knew.

MIN HOGG

A full answer would be a book in itself. A key figure was Michael Wickham, who broadened my horizons immensely (see page 39). But before I met Michael, while I was still at Central, the sculptor Eduardo Paolozzi had an enormous influence on my approach to art and design and, even more importantly, to life. Eduardo came to teach at Central after I had been there about a year. He had just come back from Paris where he had been very inspired by the work of Giacometti, Dubuffet and by the surrealists, but he was also very interested in primitive African art. In addition to sculpture, he also made collages and printed textile designs, all of which seemed to me to be bursting with originality. Later we shared a workshop in Bethnal Green where I taught him to weld. We used to visit scrapyards together where he would pick up bits and pieces of old metal to weld together for his sculptures. I have to admit that a lot of my own work at this time, particularly my textile designs, showed a heavy Paolozzi influence.

Eduardo, who was not only my teacher, but has been a lifelong friend, also gave me the first taste of a broader cultural life outside this country. He came from a family of Italian immigrants who had settled in Edinburgh where they had an ice-cream business, and I can vividly remember him introducing me to such exotic dishes as *risotto nero*, concocted from little tins of squid in their ink that his family sent down from Scotland.

Another mentor from this early period of my life was 'Den' (Douglas) Newton, a poet and expert on African art, who took me under his wing and fed me all sorts of influences, both cultural and scatological. Den Newton was actually my landlord in the early 1950s after I had left college; another tenant of Newton's who had an influence on me was the Scottish

The sculptor Eduardo Paolozzi, a lifelong inspiration and friend, and my son Sebastian.

sculptor Bill Turnbull. Ian Bradbery, a typographer who had taught at Central, became a great friend and instructed me in graphic imagery and jazz. The painter Dennis Wirth Miller similarly showed me life through his sophisticated eyes, not only art and design, but also food, wine, landscape and humour. And not least there was my first wife Brenda Davison, an experienced architect from the Cambridge school, whom I met when I lived in Warwick Gardens. Although our marriage was short-lived, I learned a lot from her about interior design and sensuality.

What were your feelings immediately after your first wife left you?

SHIRLEY CONRAN

I found it devastating at the time. I was only nineteen when we got married, which was far too young. Brenda was older than me, about twenty-four or twenty-five, and she had been married before, to a Cambridge don I think. We had already lived together for about six months before we got married and she left about five months after that. She went off with an engineer with whom she had had a previous relationship. He was later killed in a car accident in Africa.

Brenda was a very intelligent and stimulating woman, but during the time I knew her she was ill, off and on, with tuberculosis, which seemed to have quite an effect on her emotional state. I remember my mother saying to me after the marriage broke up that the next time I got married I should choose 'a nice dumb blonde'. Considering my mother was a very intelligent and well-read woman I found that an extraordinary thing to say. Perhaps it was an acknowledgement of the difficulties she herself had faced in marriage as a woman with frustrated ambitions.

Can you talk about your perceptions of American design when you were a young designer in Britain?

EAMES DEMETRIOS

When I was a student in the late 1940s, the work of your grandfather, Charles Eames, his wife Ray, and many of their contemporaries on the West Coast such as George Nelson and Alexander Girard, was our great inspiration. To which I would have to add Florence Knoll, Eero and Eliel Saarinen, Harry Bertoia and Mies van der Rohe. We learned about their work through a magazine called *Arts and Architecture* that was our design bible at the time.

Charles and Ray Eames had a huge impact on the European design world. They were inventive in so many areas: furniture, products, film, textiles, architecture, art, graphics, toys and so on. To me, their work demonstrated both an insatiable curiosity about the world and a style of life that was attainable. They seemed to offer a blueprint of how to live a better life and administered large doses of charm along the way.

Your grandfather was not merely one of my heroes as a student; his work has been an inspiration to me throughout my design career. I struggled to emulate both his ethical and aesthetic approach. His humour and intense interest in what might appear trivial to most people – such as ordinary factory components – has always been a great influence on me. I particularly like the fact that he enjoyed getting his hands dirty, really relished making things. He was a serious designer, but didn't seem to take things too seriously. This is an attitude which I hope has run through my work, too; I just wish I could have been as brilliant as he was.

Charles and Ray Eames working on a chair design. I admired their hands-on approach.

It always seemed a great pity that for a long time the work of Charles and Ray Eames almost disappeared from view in America, except perhaps in the contract furnishing market. And it is exciting that it is now getting the recognition it deserves and exerting an enormous influence once again on the design community.

You have said in the past that my father, Michael Wickham, had some influence on your early career. While I think the enthusiasm was a shared experience between you both at the time that you met, could you explain and discuss the collaboration and friendship you had with him?

JULYAN WICKHAM

I met Michael in 1951 when I was just starting out and at a very formative stage in my career. At that time he was a Condé Nast photographer and did a lot of work for *House & Garden*, where Cynthia Blackburn, whom he later married, was design editor. Cynthia and Michael had called round to the house where I was living to meet Olive Sullivan, decoration editor of *House & Garden*, who had a rosebud room in the house about as different from mine as you could imagine. They had a look in my room and asked if they could photograph my furniture, which is how we met. I found their interest in me and my ideas very flattering. Through Cynthia, my work received some of its first publicity and both were very supportive of the various directions I was exploring at the time. Michael even took up furniture-making himself.

As well as being a photographer, Michael was also a painter, musician, cook, gardener and craftsman; he wasn't a jack of all trades, he was a master of many of them, a sort of

Terence drawing at Le Bastit 1973

LEFT: *Michael Wickham, one of my best friends and greatest inspirations — a reasonably good illustrator, too.*

ABOVE: *A drawing of me by Michael, dating from 1973 and made on holiday at Le Bastit, the house I owned at that time in the Dordogne.*

pluralist approach that was immensely appealing. He was also a fund of information, much of it erudite, and extraordinarily generous with his time. His enthusiasm for the things in life that also interested me was a bond between us. He was, of course, much more experienced than I was at the time – he had lived in Spain and France before the war and knew Picasso and Braque. His politics were very left-wing (he was what you might call a 'claret communist') and he certainly didn't suffer fools gladly. Through his influence, my eyes were opened to an entirely different style of life, one that I have tried to develop and promote ever since.

One of the great turning points in my life was the trip to France we all took together in 1953. Patricia Lyttelton and I accompanied Cynthia and Michael in his wonderful old Lagonda, driving south through rural France to the Dordogne and Lot, camping out in Nancy Cunard's hayloft and various fields on the way. It was the first time I had ever been abroad and coming from austere, grey, postwar Britain I was overwhelmed by the sensual quality of everyday French life, the markets, the food in roadside cafés, the simple, unpretentious but abundant displays on stalls and in shops. The food was always delicious, washed down with carafes of rough red wine generously thrown in for free. I didn't discover these things all by myself; it was Michael who showed them to me.

Over the years Michael and I had our ups and downs, but mostly ups. I miss him greatly.

There is often a moment in early life when one's convictions are awakened or sensitized to the knowledge that a course of action will prevail and guide future activities. What event or external factors determined your own convictions and emerging activities as a designer?
DAVID CHALONER

I don't think there was one big moment of truth when I saw my future direction in life light up in front of me. Instead, I can remember lots of little triggers: the kitchens and dairies of country houses in Dorset on school visits, the work of West Coast American architects and designers illustrated in a magazine called *Arts and Architecture*, the work of Bernard Leach, sharing a workshop with Eduardo Paolozzi, reading a book about the Bauhaus, visiting the 'Britain Can Make It' exhibition at the V & A and the Milan Triennales of the early 1950s. Ironmonger's shops in France – which I first saw around the same time – had a particularly strong impact on me, and clearly demonstrated how everyday, useful things could be both practical and beautiful.

Exhibition in the shoe department of Simpson of Piccadilly, August 1952. Natasha Kroll was able to lend me the space because shoe sales were notoriously slow in August.

GETTING STARTED

My early career was a time of immense frustration. I worked extremely hard, had very little money and was always worried about cash flow. At the beginning of the 1950s, materials were still rationed and the creative and economic climate was austere; by the end of the decade, conditions were definitely changing for the better but I had not yet succeeded in presenting my ideas to a wider market.

My first and only job was working for an architect called Denis Lennon; when this came to an abrupt end in 1951, I set up on my own. I was twenty-one. My father gave me Conran and Company, the shell of his old business, and guaranteed an overdraft of £300 at the bank.

Unlike Robin Day, who had the backing of the furniture manufacturer Hille, we had to make all our own designs in a fairly unsophisticated way. Getting noticed by the right people was difficult. One of my early successes was being spotted by Natasha Kroll, the display manager of Simpson of Piccadilly, who commissioned me to design window displays and exhibited my work. There was a buyer at John Lewis called Betty Horne who also promoted my designs; and Ian MacCallum, editor of *Architectural Review*, commissioned pieces for his home and office. I sold a chair to the American architect Philip Johnson; and Picasso ordered two of my chairs after his model of the moment had been given one as a present – it consisted of a skeletal metal framework strung with rope. But my bestselling design by far was a conical terracotta pot on a metal stand.

Along with furniture design and manufacture, I designed textiles for a Lancashire company and ceramics for Midwinter. In 1953 I opened The Soup Kitchen with Ivan Storey and a year later, The Orrery, a restaurant at the 'wrong' end of the King's Road. Both ventures made a little money that I promptly invested back into

Denis Lennon, the architect for whom I worked on the 1951 Festival of Britain, gave me the opportunity to design this magazine for the rayon industry. I helped to art direct it, produced drawings for it and designed its pre-punk cover.

the furniture business. In 1956 I launched the **Conran Design Group** to provide a design service for clients – everything from exhibition displays to interiors. The design group also served as an important means of tying our various activities together; when working on a scheme for a client, we could specify our own fabrics and furniture. Most of our work at this stage was in the contract market; but by the beginning of the 1960s my ambitions were firmly focused on reaching a wider domestic audience.

Conran furniture, 1952. My bestseller at that time was a conical flowerpot on a metal stand.

Did you go to the Festival of Britain? What did you think of it?

DEYAN SUDJIC

Not only did I go to the Festival of Britain, but I worked on it and in it, sleeping on site for several weeks before it opened. I was employed by the architect Denis Lennon, who had been commissioned to work on the Transport Pavilion and the Homes and Garden Pavilion.

I designed and made furniture and textiles, designed a section of the interior of the *Princess* flying boat and helped Eduardo Paolozzi with his water sculpture. I also made three-dimensional plastic letters with entrapped shrimps, beetles, butterflies and caterpillars for F H K Henrion's Country Pavilion; the letters spelled out an exhibition heading, 'Natural World' or something like that. Unfortunately, these letters burst in the sunlight, releasing the most appalling smell, and I had to replace them with letters made of thicker plastic and get rid of the air bubbles that had caused the problem.

The Festival of Britain was a wonderful exhibition that really caught the public's imagination. It received the predictable media bashing, although not of the same intensity as the Dome. Like the Dome, it also became a political football and Churchill could not wait to demolish it; in fact, the bulldozers moved in the day it closed. For the huge number of people who saw it, it made a lasting impression and was a chink of bright and cheerful light in what was then a very grey and damaged land.

I think that those of us who worked on the Festival really expected it to open up new career possibilities and that the optimism it generated would immediately translate into orders. But rationing was still in place and the climate remained profoundly conservative. After the Festival was over, practically every architect and designer that had been involved with it ran out of work, Denis Lennon among them. He could no longer afford to employ me, so I was out of a job. I started to make furniture and did a little textile design work and also created window displays for Simpson of Piccadilly in the evenings. Life was a mixture of a certain desperation to keep financially afloat, literally to pay the gas bill, and extreme frustration in having so many ideas that nobody was interested in.

Exhibition programme for the Festival of Britain, 1951. In contrast to the excitement generated by the exhibition, the contents of the catalogue look particularly dreary and austere today.

A Dome that worked. The Dome of Discovery at the Festival of Britain, with the Skylon in the background, a London landmark that should be re-erected.

If you could choose one special vehicle what would that be, and why?

JANICE KIRKPATRICK

I think I'd choose my first ever vehicle, a pale green Vespa that I owned in the early 1950s. It got me around London so efficiently and economically and allowed me to see so much of the city that would have remained hidden to me if I'd used a more conventional means of transport.

Because it doubled up as my only delivery vehicle in the early years of my furniture-making business, the Vespa was responsible for my early experiments with KD (knockdown) or flat-pack furniture. Many of my products were too big to be transported assembled, so rather like the peripatetic medieval households with their demountable furniture, I started to experiment with the idea of making them in parts to be assembled on site.

The Vespa was also perfect for taking girls around London. These were the days before compulsory crash helmets and sitting on the back of a Vespa was a rather daring and sexy thing to do. You could tell quite a lot about a girl from the way she sat on the back. There were quite a lot of Audrey Hepburn wannabes around at the time.

The marvellous thing about Vespas is the way their design seems to encapsulate the whole flavour of that time. A few years ago Piaggio approached us with the idea that we might develop a Vespa café with them. We met the charming Giovanni Agnelli who was running the company and discussed the project and how to roll it out around the world.

We designed a prototype for the café using masses of Vespa memorabilia, but tried to bring the aesthetic up to date so that it didn't look like a themed restaurant. I'm sure the idea could have been a great success, but unfortunately Giovanni died tragically and the project died with him.

Although they are not Vespa places, the Carluccio's Caffès, which my sister and her husband Antonio have opened very successfully, make use of many of the same elements and promote the friendliness of the archetypal cafés that were a feature of every Italian town in the 1950s.

Which three books do you most remember reading in your twenties?

NORMAN FOSTER

Mechanization Takes Command by Siegfried Giedion, which inspired me to understand how mass production of design was possible; Vile Bodies by Evelyn Waugh, which amused me greatly and made me see the disadvantages of social privilege; and A Book of Mediterranean Food by Elizabeth David, which made me aware that there was a much better style of life waiting to be tasted across the Channel.

How well do you remember Sir Gordon Russell? How would you rate him as a designer, manufacturer, pioneering modernist shopkeeper and, most importantly, as a design theorist through his work with Utility furniture and later as director of the Council of Industrial Design?

Would you agree that Gordon Russell's belief in simplicity of form, honesty of materials, respect for both hand- and machine-making, together with a certain tweediness of outlook, was the major influence on British design as it developed in the mid-twentieth century?

And, if so, do you feel in retrospect that this was a good or bad thing?

FIONA MacCARTHY

To remind myself about Gordon Russell, I pulled down a few books about him and read in particular a speech he made on 13 December 1956 at the Royal Society of Arts. I was struck by the fact that practically everything he said then is still relevant today; in 1956, his views must have sounded quite revolutionary.

Gordon Russell was director of the CoID at a pivotal moment, when the artist-craftsmen of the Arts and Crafts movement were giving way to the industrial designers of the machine age, and he did a wonderful job, with great intellect and energy, trying to bridge that gap. I always felt that while his heart remained in Broadway, in that Cotswolds world of crafts and rural pursuits, his head clearly understood the changing nature of industrialized society and that design was no longer just an elitist career for Fabian gentlemen (or women).

The CoID had been established in 1944 to promote design and co-ordinate design activities. It had close links with the Board of Trade, a connection intended to encourage manufacturers, retailers and wholesalers to use designers and to convince them not only that well-designed products might sell, they might even sell better than products that no one had applied much thought to. I suppose it was really trying to give everybody 'good taste'.

Gordon Russell's speech to the RSA is particularly interesting because it evokes the difficult context in which designers found themselves in the postwar years and because it clearly expresses a vision of the role design might play in society, an ideal that many of us at the time seemed to absorb by osmosis. In the speech he states that designers 'owe a duty not only to the manufacturers who make the goods they design but to the public who use them', and says that designers can raise their status by 'raising the quality, including design in its widest sense, of all industrial products, bringing the artist in many different ways back into the main stream of life from which he has been absent too long, to our and his great loss'. He concludes by saying, 'This will not only improve the standard of living of every man, woman and child in this country, but it will enhance our prestige abroad and thus, to our advantage, profoundly affect our competitive position in the markets of the world.'

I have no difficulty with the sentiments, but the aspect that worried me most at the time was the rather paternalistic, elitist nature of British design immediately before and after the war. The whole design world seemed to consist of a lot of frightfully nice chaps who belonged to the best clubs and who were all terribly concerned about the 'appalling' taste of the working class. This general attitude was enshrined in the Faculty of Royal Designers for Industry and the whole idea of patronage. It always seemed as if the CoID had to apply moral blackmail to industrialists to persuade them to employ a designer at all. The unspoken threat was that the King/Queen/Prince Philip would never visit a manufacturer's factory or exhibition stand if they didn't engage the services of a 'royal' designer.

In the mid-1950s I became a member of the Society of Industrial Artists, which is what designers were called in those days. There were strict rules that members should not compete with each other. Our newly formed design group comprised about six or seven designers at that time and I started to think about how we should market our services. I decided that we should publish a simple newsletter describing the work we had done and send it out to potential clients.

One day, I received a phone call from the secretary of the Society, asking me to go and see him, as there had been a complaint about our activities from one of the other members. When I turned up, he produced one of our news-sheets as if it were a discarded fish and chip wrapper and asked why we had sent it to a client of one of 'his' members. Did I not realize that it was against the rules of the Society to solicit work in this way?

I explained that I had to find ways of getting work for my small team in order to pay their wages. I asked him how he suggested I went about this. He told me to join a club – the Travellers, the Athenaeum or Boodles, for example. 'Get to know people, old boy, have a drink with them and you might get some work. That's how our members do it.'

I was so appalled by this that I continued to produce the newsletters and consequently was thrown out of the Society. I was later asked to rejoin when it had become the Society of Industrial Artists and Designers and had embraced the notion that it really was quite a good idea for its members to promote their own businesses and expand their influence.

Gordon Russell was certainly a very courteous gentleman, not an angry young man like me. He set some very decent standards of Britishness and quality in his work and the Utility furniture ranges were a lesson to us all. The RSA speech is also very revealing when it comes to his own taste for simplicity: '... what one sees is profoundly affected by what one does not see. A good sculptor is always aware of the bone structure.' He disparages the use of design as superficial styling, its role in creating a 'craze for novelty' and the proliferation of what he calls 'signatures' but what I suppose we would now call 'logos'. He criticizes designers who adopt modernist aesthetics without reference to real needs, but he also reminds those engineers who are not interested in aesthetics that 'It seldom costs more to use a good shape instead of a bad one ...' Utility restrictions, which had prohibited decoration in furniture and ceramics for ten years, were lifted in 1952, opening the floodgates and, like many people, Russell was apparently concerned that designers might stray from the path of simplicity and functional quality. But I never really felt that austerity came naturally to him; he was not Jasper Morrison at heart. His real passion, indeed, seemed to be building stone walls, which says something very nice about him.

Two of my fabric designs, circa 1954. I'd like to reprint 'Leaf' again. I don't know where the obelisk came from!

The formidable Elizabeth David, doyenne of food writers, in her kitchen.

I recently spent time with someone who had worked closely with Elizabeth David. He confirmed, as was apparent from a recent television programme, that she was a colourful character. You have said that she was a great culinary inspiration to you. Can you elaborate?
WENDY JONES

Elizabeth David was far more than a culinary inspiration, although she was certainly that as well. For those of us who were young in the immediate postwar years she let a beam of strong sunlight into the gloomy life of grey, rationed Britain and showed us that just across the Channel there was another style of life that was far more delicious than anything our generation had ever experienced.

Although Elizabeth David chiefly wrote about food, she wrote about it in such a way that you sat up in bed reading her books and licking your lips, as if you were reading a salacious novel. In a way, that's exactly what her books were. The style of life that she described seemed impossibly remote, but you longed to experience it. Fifty years later, many of us have now tasted what she described and have incorporated many of the qualities she wrote about into our own lives in this country, and we are much the better for it.

I met Elizabeth David a few times and she was certainly not the easiest person. We were introduced by her good friend Walter Baxter, whose restaurant, The Chanterelle, I designed in the late 1950s. My second wife Shirley was very keen to ask her to supper and so we did. It was a fairly tense meal. Shirley and Elizabeth David didn't exactly hit it off. I think we ate egg mayonnaise, with anchovies drooped over the top to start with; I certainly remember insisting that we served something simple, nothing too complicated that we might get wrong.

All of us are influenced by past experiences. Who or what was your biggest influence?
RAYMOND BLANC

In terms of food and eating out, the atmosphere of French restaurants, particularly the large Parisian brasseries, have been a great influence on me. Before I opened my Soup Kitchens I spent some time in the early 1950s working as a *plongeur*, or washer-up, in La Méditerranée in Paris to learn about the restaurant business from the inside. It was an eye-opening experience; the squalid kitchen conditions and casual brutality of the chefs came as a great shock. But something about the whole theatre of restaurant life got into my bloodstream and has stayed there ever since.

In the mid-1950s, I was brave enough to have lunch at La Pyramide, Fernand Point's restaurant in Vienne. This was my first introduction to *haute cuisine*. Soon afterwards, I went to Madame Barattero, a small restaurant recommended by Elizabeth David in a small town called Lamastre. The food was the best I have ever eaten, not *haute cuisine*, not regional, but utterly delicious. Madame sat outside her restaurant, topping and tailing huge piles of fine green beans with a friend, and keeping a beady eye on the fresh produce being delivered to her restaurant.

I had *poulet en vessie*, a whole chicken cooked in a pig's bladder, with finely sliced truffles stuffed under the breast. When the 'football' was punctured, the whole restaurant filled with the most appetizing aroma I have ever smelled. We had the remains of the chicken cold the next day and this was even better.

Where and when did you first eat foie gras?
KASMIN

I first ate proper foie gras in Paris in 1954. I was with Mark Birley, who had asked me to design a little Hermès shop in Piccadilly Arcade. On the same occasion, I also tasted a bit of black truffle. Both experiences made a lasting and expensive impression on me. Every Christmas my mother used to get sent a pot of foie gras from one of my father's friends; it was more like liver paste with a tasteless black cube in the middle masquerading as a truffle to the uninitiated. Not at all the same thing.

You've done a lot to promote British food and ingredients in your restaurants, but what is your favourite London greasy spoon caff?
KEN LIVINGSTONE

My youth was spent in a marvellous transport caff on the King's Road called The Cosy. It had high-backed narrow benches, was filled with steam and cigarette smoke and served huge mugs of sweet tea and large plates of rashers of back bacon, fried eggs, fried bread and bubble and squeak in generous quantities, all for about a shilling. Coffee was Camp, the concentrated essence stuff from a bottle. Sometimes we had two oak-smoked kippers or a large smoked haddock, with a couple of poached eggs and wonderful flabby bread spread with dripping on the side.

There aren't many of these places left, sadly, because the health and safety police insist on such ridiculous standards of clinical correctness. Instead of greasy spoons we've got McBurgerbars, which deeply offend my taste buds in practically every way. I would, however, recommend an eel and pie shop called Manze's in Tower Bridge Road, about five minutes' walk from your new cocoon. You could take John Prescott – I'm sure *he* would recognize mushy peas as mushy peas!

What was the London restaurant scene like in the year before you opened The Soup Kitchen?
LOYD GROSSMAN

Around the time we opened the first Soup Kitchen in 1953 restaurant-goers had very little choice indeed. On the one hand, there were the cheap Lyons Corner Houses and the British Restaurants. (For those who don't remember them, 'British Restaurants', and they really were called by that name, were subsidized canteens that came in during the war years.) At the

French café society in the early 1950s, as I remember it. I used to sit around with Christopher Logue and his friends who were writing pornography for the Olympus Press to make ends meet.

other end of the spectrum there were the expensive Frenchified places that my friends and I certainly couldn't afford. In Soho and its environs there were a few more reasonable places, such as Bianchi's, Bertorelli's, Schmidt's and Boulestin, but these were rarities.

Generally, the average restaurant-goer faced a fairly depressing prospect. Most food was mass-produced: Telfers meat pies, tasteless breadcrumb sausages and dark brown gravy was the norm. If you ordered a salad you usually got an undressed plate of hard-boiled eggs, sliced on a gadget and stained with chopped beetroot, a few large spring onions, some outer leaves of lettuce and maybe a bit of scraped old carrot. Spam cropped up all over the place and was more palatable as a fritter. Mashed potatoes were always watery and lumpy and might have had a bit of margarine added; vegetables were overcooked and grey; and sandwiches, which were staple fare, consisted of two slices of processed bread that might have a sliver of ham passed between them. Chips were always limp and very greasy. You ate because you were hungry, not for pleasure, and drank beer and Merrydown cider with dire morning-after consequences. A glass of wine was seen as quite radical and rather arty.

As people who enjoyed good food and drink but didn't have a great deal of money to spend on eating out, we thought our Soup Kitchen idea seemed a logical response to a glaring gap in the market. The Soup Kitchen menu consisted of four kinds of soup, French bread, cheddar cheese, real coffee (we had one of the first Gaggia machines in London) and apple tart, all cheap, wholesome and filling; equally important, given our relative lack of experience in the restaurant business, by limiting the fare we avoided having to employ a chef.

Do you miss your old Soup Kitchen days?

ANNA FORD

I certainly miss being twenty-two and I miss the simplicity of being able to do things in a naive way that sidestepped bureaucracy – being able to make a decision and get on with it. I don't miss the austerity of those days or the tiny audience for anything I did. Nor do I miss the dismal process of trying to persuade bankers, who wanted to see my absurd new-fangled ideas fail, to lend me a couple of quid.

I do remember the opening of our first Soup Kitchen as a terrific highlight. We had sent out flyers advertizing our new venture and, when the day came, we threw open our doors at midday and waited expectantly for customers. Instead, about forty tramps shambled in under the misapprehension that we were running a charity. We didn't have the heart to send them away, fed them all a bowl of soup and watched our cash flow projections go down the drain. A journalist who had come along for the opening knew a good story when she saw one and wrote up the incident for the evening paper. That evening the entire cast of *Guys and Dolls*, the musical opening that same night, turned up out of curiosity and after that The Soup Kitchen became the trendy place to go. It was so successful, in fact, that we

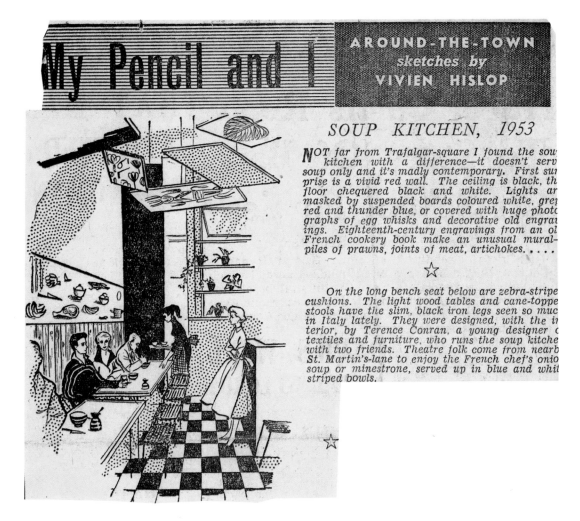

Illustration by Vivien Hislop of The Soup Kitchen, the restaurant I opened with Ivan Storey in 1953. Ivan found the premises in Chandos Place and raised the funding; I designed the interior. This sketch appeared in the Evening News, *along with a write-up.*

opened several more, including one in Cambridge, where I learned my first important lesson in table-turning. The Cambridge Soup Kitchen became a mecca for students lingering for hours over one coffee, which was disastrous in terms of takings.

The year after we opened the first Soup Kitchen, I opened a slightly more ambitious restaurant called The Orrery, opposite Bluebird garage in the King's Road. This time I did employ a chef; he was Polish, very eccentric, and used to sleep on the ice-cream fridge at night. There was an area at the back of the restaurant which I paved with York stone flags and where I set up an outdoor grill. That summer was particularly fine and sunny and people flocked to eat outdoors in the shade of the plane trees.

In a way, I'm sorry I didn't stick with Soup Kitchens; I should have seen at the time that there was something there, a real opportunity to produce good, cheap, everyday food. But I wasn't really a restaurateur then; the Soup Kitchen enterprise was a means to an end, a way to make some money for my furniture-making business.

Speaking as a man who's been married four times, I would like to know what it was like being married to Superwoman. Pros and cons.

BARRY HUMPHRIES

Speaking as a man who's also been married four times . . . Shirley the Superwoman was very beautiful, very flirtatious and very ambitious. I met her in my café in the King's Road, The Orrery, in about 1954; she was with David Queensberry whom she wanted to marry, as she was keen to be a marchioness. Why she left him for me is one of life's great mysteries. At the time of our marriage a year later I was rather shy and still a failure financially. 'Shows promise' was probably the best that could have been said of me.

Shirley was then quite a gentle person; she'd had a fairly unhappy upbringing and, like me, had rather a difficult father who could be quite violent. She'd been to art school and after we married she worked with me on the textile side of the business.

In the early years of our marriage I was busy trying to be successful making furniture and from the outset Shirley seemed to believe that it was her role to publicize my work. I hated publicity, especially of the personal variety: it went against everything I believed in at that time. I just wanted to get on with my work, keep a low profile and not be exposed; I was very shy indeed. Shirley thoroughly believed in PR and was good at it. She maintained, quite rightly, that I wouldn't get anywhere without it. The whole issue became quite a source of conflict between us.

Although we lived an outwardly glamorous life, we were always very broke. Our house was in Regent's Park Terrace, Camden Town, and was part of a terrace of twenty-two houses that had been restored. Before our marriage I had bought a ninety-nine-year lease for £4,250. We couldn't afford to live in all of the house, so we rented out part as a flat, and for a time I had my office in another part. This part of London was heavily colonized by what we would now call the 'chattering classes'; our garden backed onto the gardens of Jonathan Miller and David Gentleman. Life in NW1 in those days was indeed just like Mark Boxer's later satire, 'The Stringalongs'.

We worked very hard, had a pretty good time and a couple of decent kids. Our social life, however, was far from exciting; we tended to stay in and entertain at home when we could. Shirley was keen to get on and keen to get into society; I think she felt we were missing out, particularly since friends like Mary Quant and Alexander Plunket Greene, who were much more successful at the time, seemed to spend every evening at parties and restaurants.

Around the end of the 1950s my design group began to work with Harveys of Bristol. Joy, the wife of my client, George McWatters, was employed on the *Daily Mail* and she became very friendly with Shirley and introduced her to journalism. Shirley already had ambitions in this area; she saw it as a glamorous world where she could really make a name for herself. I felt that her ambitions started to overtake her life; at any rate, they provided the usual potential for conflict.

A series of photographs of Shirley and me, taken in 1955, out on the town and at home in Regent's Park Terrace. The open display unit was the divider between the kitchen and dining room (BELOW RIGHT); the whole family – me, Shirley and Sebastian – at breakfast (BELOW FAR RIGHT). At that time, Shirley was a great advocate of personal publicity, while I was very much against it.

We eventually separated in 1962; Shirley left and went off to live in the house of a friend. In the meantime, I found myself with space to let in the house and Dinah Herbert (later Morrison), who had been my secretary for four years, suggested her sister, Caroline, as a tenant. Caroline moved into Regent's Park Terrace with her boyfriend, but quite soon afterwards split up with him and started going out with me.

Like Shirley, Caroline was also a journalist and had worked for *House & Garden* and *Queen* magazine. When she was at *Queen*, Jocelyn Stevens named Radio Caroline after her, as he saw her as the archetypal young listener. She was altogether a steadier person than Shirley and more containably ambitious.

Shirley got the Regent's Park Terrace house as part of the divorce settlement in 1963; Caroline and I left and she moved back in. Not too long afterwards she married John Stephenson, who was the director of my design group, and that proved to be a very awkward time indeed. It was so awkward that John left the company (returning later after he had broken up with Shirley).

Caroline and I also got married and set up home first in a damp basement near Primrose Hill, then in Fitzroy Square and finally, several years later, in a superb 1820s house designed by Decimus Burton in St Andrew's Place, Regent's Park, which was riddled with a very active form of dry rot. It was arguably the best address in London, even if the house was falling down around our ears, and it had the advantage of being just down the road from the old Regent's Park Terrace house where my sons were living with Shirley.

Shirley, of course, went on to become a very successful journalist, especially after her 'Superwoman' idea took off, and subsequently a bestselling novelist. We have remained friends – off and on – over the many years since then. Incidentally, I gave her the idea for the goldfish scene in *Lace* after going to a midsummer party in Finland by the side of a lake.

What wisdom – if any – did Vivien Leigh offer you?

NICOLE SWENGLEY

Vivien Leigh came to the first night of a restaurant I designed in the 1950s; it was called The Chanterelle and was run by Walter Baxter, who was a well-known writer at the time. The design featured a lot of natural wood, but there were hanging lamps over each table. She took objection to these and pointed out that the most attractive forms of lighting were footlights directed so that there are no harsh shadows on the face. Walter Baxter suggested that I paint the insides of the shades pink to warm the tone of the lighting up a bit.

After this episode, we were all having lunch at John Fowler's house in the country and my son Sebastian picked a large bunch of dandelions and presented them to Vivien as an apology for his father lighting her lovely face so badly.

We know that you had restaurants in London in the 1950s but did your interest in wine and passion for Burgundy begin before then?

BILL BAKER

My interest in wine dates from the late 1950s when I worked as a design consultant for Harveys of Bristol. I designed a restaurant for the company in their wonderful cellars and used to attend wine tastings with my client, Michael Broadbent, and Harry Waugh when they were putting together their amazing list. This was really the first time I tasted old red Burgundies and the experience convinced me that if and when I could ever afford such wines, they would be my first choice.

I am thirty now and trying to plan the future of my studio and balance ambitions with practical choices. I am curious about what kind of perspective you had on your future when you were thirty and how your dreams compare to where you are now.

THOMAS HEATHERWICK

I was your age in 1961 and it was a turning point in my life too. Maybe one's thirtieth birthday is the moment when you feel you have got to think seriously about the future for the first time and maybe it's also the time when you realize that you really are an adult, with adult responsibilities.

I have always found it difficult to plan ahead, particularly having lived through the war as a child. The immediate postwar years were not much better, and any plan you made seemed to get overthrown by events outside one's control. When I was in my twenties no one seemed to have any money and even if they did there was very little to spend it on. More seriously from my point of view, nobody seemed to want to employ designers or be interested in what they designed, especially if they were young, inexperienced and rather shy like I was.

My first proper workshop was a derelict three-storey warehouse, Donne Place in Chelsea, but I had no showcase for my work and I realized that my light was going to stay under a bushel unless I found a public place for it to shine. I started with a basement showroom under a flower shop in the Piccadilly Arcade, moved on to an old stable building in Cadogan Lane and from there to a Jewish Charitable School in Hanway Place, at the corner of Oxford Street and Tottenham Court Road. This marvellous building had been bomb-damaged and needed major conversion work but it provided a perfect space for a showroom and design offices.

Meanwhile, our workshop had moved to North End Road, Fulham, to the premises of an old forage merchant owned by a pair of brothers who were running out of horses to feed in London. A little later we established our first woodworking factory in Cock Yard,

Camberwell, another derelict building that had been a horse bus garage and more recently a jam factory.

All this time the business was growing, not at an astronomical rate, but pretty steadily. I had established myself in the contract furniture market, and my design group was increasingly successful. By the early 1960s we were growing out of our ramshackle factories in Fulham and Camberwell and desperately needed more space. The year I turned thirty saw me planning to move from my workshops in London to a purpose-built factory in Thetford, Norfolk and designing and prototyping my first ranges of domestic furniture. I was fairly firmly set on an expansionary course, only to be blown off it several times as the decade progressed.

If I could have dreamt at thirty about how my life would proceed over the next forty years, I simply would not have believed it. When I was the age you are now, designers had virtually no profile and were regarded as unfundable. One of the things I never imagined was the extent to which design would become part of everyday cultural life. Today, people make television programmes about design in all its forms; design is part of the National Curriculum and designers themselves are household names. There may be further to go; the critical role the creative industries have to play in the future of the economy is still not fully recognized by government, but the situation now is infinitely more promising than it was then.

I believe that if you can isolate those things that you want to achieve, you will be able to make them happen because you live in a world that respects and can afford your remarkable talents. An important consideration for future development would be the extent to which you are prepared to let work dominate you life. I suspect, rather like me, your work is also your pleasure and every moment you are not working you view as wasted time. But only you can determine that balance.

We started out together in Soho at about the same time in the 1950s. You have made a great success of your business life but there must have been moments of crisis. What was the worst?

MICHAEL HESELTINE

I've had quite a few moments of crisis, as indeed you have too, but one of the worst I can remember, probably because it was the first really serious one, came in 1961 when I had committed to moving eighty families to Thetford in Norfolk. We had planned the move with their enthusiastic agreement but they suddenly started to get cold feet.

At this point we had already sold our factories in London to take advantage of the Expanding Town Scheme, an initiative that sponsored businesses to move out of London; our new factory, offices and showroom in Thetford were not yet complete. Under the scheme, London County Council in partnership with Thetford had agreed to provide new homes for our staff.

ABOVE: *Our design company produced one of the first corporate identity manuals in Britain for Harveys of Bristol in the early 1960s. The manual showed the company how to monitor its image.*

LEFT: *Our design for an early Harveys off-licence. The wine trade was very conservative in those days, dominated by old Masters of Wine who could never conceive that wine might one day be sold in a supermarket.*

RIGHT: *One of the Lavender brothers at his desk in the forage merchant in North End Road, Fulham, which became our workshop.*

ABOVE AND ABOVE RIGHT: *Our new factory and showroom at Thetford, Norfolk, 1962, inside and out.*

Then scare stories started to appear in the local papers about the new houses; there were reports of 'rats as big as dogs' overrunning the estate and claims that the door locks froze in cold weather. People started to come to me and say that 'the wife has decided that we won't move out of London next spring'. The situation escalated alarmingly until about half of the families who had previously decided to move reneged on their agreements. This was a serious crisis and would certainly have bankrupted our business.

We had to tackle the problem head-on. With the help of the LCC and the excellent Thetford town clerk, we organized another trip to Norfolk so the families could see the situation for themselves. Luckily, on the day of the outing it was fine and sunny and the new houses looked particularly good. It turned out that the 'rats' were actually coypus that lived in the local woods. We were also able to demonstrate that all the door locks needed was a little oil to stop them freezing. By then the new factory was nearly finished and this looked quite spectacular compared with our old ramshackle premises back in London. After some large cups of tea and pints of local beer, an inspiring talk by the town clerk and a dose of sympathy, the families were back on side; they even sang in the buses on the way home. Eventually, eighty families made the move and only ten per cent returned to London.

HABITAT

The first Habitat opened in the Fulham Road on 11 May 1964. It was far from an impulsive venture. I'd spent the previous decade trying to get my work in front of the public and had come to the conclusion that the direct approach was the only way. Maurice Libby and Katie Currie, like-minded people whom I had met through a shop called Woollands, came to work with me; my wife Caroline shared responsibility for the kitchen department; an ex-model called Pagan Taylor was shop manager. Another key figure was Oliver Gregory, who worked on the design and conversion of the shop. He was a trained joiner as well as a designer and had come to work with me at the Design Group. Oliver had a keen appreciation of how things were actually made and shared my aesthetic.

In those days, Fulham Road was off the beaten track. The premises I found were opposite the Michelin Building in an area now known as Brompton Cross; there was a large basement as well as a ground floor, which made the rent rather attractive. We put in a huge shop window and converted it very simply with white walls and a quarry-tiled floor; I think the whole fit-out cost £6,000. The shop was stocked with our own furniture and fabric designs and with dozens of household products, everything from chopping boards to paper lanterns. People don't buy major items of furniture very frequently, so the idea was to entice customers to return by offering the opportunity to make smaller, more casual purchases. I remember saying that customers should brush up against the furniture like cows until they got used to it.

The directors of the first Habitat, photographed for the Sunday Times *by Terry Donovan in May 1964.*

I remember some of our staff being quite mystified by my insistence that the crockery, cookware and other items be displayed stacked high, as if they were in a warehouse. I was trying to create that irresistible feeling of plenty you find on market stalls; to begin with, my display staff kept trying to arrange things 'artistically'. But the stacked displays became quite a distinctive feature of Habitat and served to draw in the crowds, just as I had hoped. We weren't an instant financial success, but critically speaking we were definitely in the right place at the right time. Habitat has been called the first 'lifestyle' shop, but I'm not sure that's a compliment.

In the beginning, I only imagined Habitat would be one shop. But our early success and the lack of response from anyone else in the retail business convinced me that I could expand the idea into a chain. Two years after the first Habitat, we opened a second London branch in Tottenham Court Road; we had three branches more, in Manchester, Kingston and Bromley, by 1968.

What do you consider to be your greatest achievement?
SEBASTIAN CONRAN

Starting Habitat.

Sixties' street scene in 'swinging' London.

As someone who is often cited as a catalyst for the 'Swinging Sixties', were you aware that you were living in an extraordinary period?

ALICE RAWSTHORN

I don't think that any of us were really aware of the changes that were taking place at the time, changes that with the benefit of hindsight we can now see were quite radical. Most of us just got on with trying to make things happen and make ends meet. Because it was so difficult to persuade people in positions of power that our ideas were saleable, it drove many of us to open shops of our own; this was really the only way we could reach customers who might like what we had to offer. Looking back, it is more obvious that by setting our own fashion, making and selling products that other young people wanted, not recycling those of an older generation, we initiated a minor revolution in taste and retailing.

What people forget about London in the 1960s is just how limited this 'revolution' actually was – the fashion scene was restricted to a few key streets (Carnaby Street, the King's Road and Kensington High Street) and promoted by a few key people, retailers, photographers and designers, most of whom knew each other.

I knew Mary Quant, for example, very well; I'd been at school with her husband, Alexander. Her first shop, Bazaar, had opened in the King's Road in 1955; two years later she had found another space for a second shop, a unit in a new building in Knightsbridge Green (a building, incidentally, that is currently being rebuilt). Opening this shop in the middle of Knightsbridge was an incredibly brave step; there was a world of difference between the boutiques of the King's Road and the rather grander retailing environment of Knightsbridge. A student architect friend of Alexander's had designed the first Bazaar but neglected to get planning permission, which caused them some difficulties; this time Mary asked me to do it. In the event, I not only designed the shop, but my Contracts company built it as well.

It was a hugely exciting job. Mary and Bazaar were very much in the limelight and it was my first real shop design. I decided to make the whole of the shopfront entirely out of glass so that passers-by could see straight in – and I remember worrying frantically whether we could actually get a piece of glass that was big enough to fit the frontage. Inside, we designed a mezzanine or balcony level with open stairs leading down to the ground floor and hung great bales of fabric on the walls. Mary's idea was to use the shop as a venue for fashion shows as well as retailing; the models used to change on the mezzanine, walk down the staircase and then parade the length of the shop. With the glass frontage, all this activity was visible from the street, which was not the way shops were usually designed in those days. The shop became the centre of all of Mary's activities and was always buzzing with people, models and photographers, partygoers and hangers-on as well as actual customers.

This was taking place a few years before the press invented the 'swinging' tag, but the genesis of it was there in that small community. When the 1960s got under way and the media attention increased, one thing we were constantly told was that what we were doing was only relevant to our small arty area of London and was of very little interest to people outside it – except, perhaps, Liverpool (because of the Beatles). Most of us didn't believe this, which was why, after the critical success of the first Habitat in Fulham Road, I opened branches in Tottenham Court Road, Glasgow, Manchester and Brighton as quickly as I could.

In the 1960s, when I was a student at the Royal College, Paul Reilly's Design Council was the only place you could go to see contemporary design. So to walk into Habitat then was an extraordinary and marvellous experience. But I remember thinking, 'Are there really enough design cognoscenti about to buy all this brave new design?'

What I have just said will sound extraordinary to anyone who didn't experience the 1950s and '60s. But in the context of postwar austere Britain, with tacky furniture shops selling pale imitations of Danish furniture and no primary colours, what you did was a brave revolution.

The more so because in Britain nobody was practising good design as the heart of a successful business. There were no good design retailers and there were no manufacturers with conspicuously well-designed products. When Jeremy Fry and I were just starting to make a go of the Rotork Sea Truck high-speed landing craft (winner of the Duke of Edinburgh's Designers Prize, 1975), I remember saying that 'if Terence can found a successful business based on good design, then so can we'. What you did was inspirational to so many of us.

Why did you feel that you could design household goods for a British public that was clearly showing no signs of being interested? Or was it a type of gamble and a desire to do the impossible? Or did you feel capable, in a pied piper manner, of so influencing a large enough London clientele?

JAMES DYSON

As you have so dramatically illustrated with your own products, people can only buy what they are offered. And they often don't know what they want until it is put under their noses at a price they can afford.

For me, Habitat was just like that. In the early 1960s, I was a medium-sized furniture manufacturer, successful at selling contract furniture via architects to commercial users such as universities, offices and hotels; I also designed and manufactured textiles and ran quite a well-established design group. On the furniture side, I became increasingly convinced that there was a great opportunity to sell my designs to the domestic market. What I hadn't fully realized at that time was that the product was not enough by itself.

When we produced our Summa range of flat-packed furniture in 1962 we needed retailers and their staff to demonstrate our enthusiasm for the designs. By and large they

Mary Quant's shop Bazaar in Knightsbridge, which we designed and built in the late 1950s.

didn't, and our domestic products looked entirely out of place in their dreary shops. The retailers could not see the world was changing and were too lazy and complacent to seize the opportunity.

The one glowing exception to this lack of vision was Woollands, a store in Knightsbridge near what is now Harvey Nichols and very like Harvey Nichols in concept. At Woollands, the managing director Martin Moss ran a small furniture department that stocked our designs. The furniture was intelligently arranged in room settings to give people an idea of how they might work in their homes and the sales staff were very knowledgeable and enthusiastic. Our success at Woollands was not enough to generate the kind of turnover our business needed, but it did prove to me that our domestic designs would sell, given the right context.

Hence our Habitat experiment. I suppose you could say it was our 'student demo'. Part of the motivation was frustration. I had become a bit of an angry young man and the more frustrated I became, the more determined I was to prove 'them' wrong. But another part of the motivation was a real conviction, shared by myself and my friends, that a better style of life should be more widely available. Habitat showed that you need to follow the same philosophy right through from drawing board, via manufacturing, to the retail shop floor. The message must be clear and uncontaminated. This is what Habitat achieved in the 1960s and what you achieve today.

Room sets showing our
Summa range of
domestic furniture, 1962.
The only store to present
our products in an
imaginative way was
Woollands, a department
store in Knightsbridge.
This was due to Martin
Moss, the inspirational
managing director, and
David Phillips, the buyer
who later joined us at
Habitat.

One day in the 1960s my wife said to me, 'You must see a new wonderful shop in the Fulham Road called Habitat.' Some months later we had decided that civil engineering was too dull and so we decided to make some changes. Our company became a supplier to Habitat and later to The Conran Shop, and still is today.

The opening of that one shop in those days was something so new and inspiring that my question to you would be: among your many achievements, was setting up the first Habitat your finest?

JOHN LUBAOWSKI

Habitat certainly got my name and ideas in front of the public. It was not an immediate financial success (our turnover at the end of the first year was £62,000 – just about what we take on a normal Saturday afternoon in The Conran Shop these days – and our first net profit was £1,649) but we gained an important degree of recognition more or less straight away.

Habitat became the public repository for the products I had already designed and the opportunity to source and present others to the public, such as good practical cookware, china and glass. In the late 1950s, early 1960s, practically the only place in London where you could buy proper pots, pans and knives – not nasty, flimsy, tinny junk – was a tiny shop in Covent Garden called Madame Cadec. Elizabeth David had written very vividly about pots and pans; I was certainly doing a lot of cooking myself by that time and was very interested in the idea of supplying decent kitchen equipment.

When we opened Habitat, I was determined that we should have a really good kitchen department. I found a wonderful wholesaler in Les Halles (still there today) called Dehillerin and their range of stock became the basis of the Habitat kitchen department. Quite soon after we opened, Elizabeth David came into the shop and bought a load of things. When she was paying at the desk, the assistant noticed that one of the knives she had picked out was bent a bit at the tip and that it still had a label with the maker's name (we normally removed the labels). The assistant offered to get another knife from the stockroom, but Miss David assured her that it was perfectly fine, that it didn't matter. When we later heard that she was setting up her own shop, the penny dropped. It had been the label she was interested in; she was sourcing things for her own shop. I think this was one of the greatest compliments anyone has ever paid me.

I also remember very well the day when you came into the shop with some examples of glass and enamelware that you had brought back from a family visit to Poland and asked whether I was interested in them. I was: these products had just the sort of robust quality that we were looking for and as soon as we stocked them they quickly became identified with the Habitat look, the enamelware in particular. You became not only our favourite glass supplier but a major supplier of Polish glass worldwide.

I think what made Habitat one of the first 'lifestyle' shops (ugh, what a horrible word) was this look, the fact that all the products appeared to have been selected by one pair of eyes. We had a shared philosophy and the staff were as passionate about the products we sold as I was.

Habitat did for the home what fashion designers like Mary Quant, Foale & Tuffin, Barbara Hulanicki and Ossie Clarke were doing for clothing. When we opened in 1964 we were part of a minor revolution in taste, instigated by young people who for the first time had a small amount of money in their pockets.

I gained huge satisfaction from seeing my ideas win public acceptance. But my 'finest moments' are really seeing something that I have designed – whether it be a piece of furniture, a shop, hotel or restaurant interior, or a piece of china or glass – in its final form.

In your years as a retailer of 'continental' style, have you seen yourself as an assimilator of 'other' Western taste, bringing style to the British public?
ANOUSKA HEMPEL

I've never really thought of myself as a retailer of continental style, although it's fair to say that I was very influenced in the early days of Habitat by what I saw in shops and markets in France and northern Italy. Since then the style has developed into what those outside Britain seem to recognize as an eclectic British style, but I know to be made up of products culled from every corner of the world. These products pass through our buyers' educated sieves and then end up looking as if they have been chosen by a single person.

Merchandising meetings in the early days of Habitat were some of the most stimulating I can remember. Buyers would present the products they had sourced and we would all argue about their respective merits, aesthetic, economic and practical. Things could get rather heated on occasion, but it was far from a cynical exercise; people did believe passionately in what they were selling.

As a retailer, what is the best product you have ever sold?
GEORGIA GLYNN SMITH

The duvet, as it was symbolic of social change. We had sold duvets in Habitat stores in Britain and decided to include them in the range when we opened in France. A lot of people were sceptical, because the French were accustomed to sheets and blankets. But I thought we really ought to give it a try. Our promotion '20 secondes pour faire un lit!' was a huge success and undoubtedly changed the sex life of Europe.

PREVIOUS PAGES: *I've always been inspired by the sight of goods piled high on market stalls and in old-fashioned ironmongers. Our kitchen in London today* (LEFT) *reveals my love of practical, useful things. Just the sort of products Habitat sold along with furniture in its early days* (RIGHT).

Habitat's '20-second bed' – the duvet doing its bit for feminism and the sex life of Europe. The (male) model is Roger Evans, then Habitat's furniture buyer.

How could interior design and merchandising play a contributing role in economic development in the Third World?

RAYMUND KÖNIGK

Design, when it is combined with good craftsmanship and a low labour cost, can certainly help the economic development of a Third World country. So often you see excellent craftsmanship and materials being wasted on badly designed objects that never achieve good home or export prices. Designers have to know the taste, style and quality expected in overseas markets and also need to work closely with craftspeople to develop their skills.

Working with sophisticated overseas markets can help the development of the home market as expectations are gradually raised. Never forget that the design of a product should retain a national characteristic that should aim to be a desirable and unique component. This is where design has a major part to play in identifying the skills, materials and aesthetic quality that belong to and can be identified as coming from a particular country. Intelligent design is undoubtedly the most economic method of adding value to a product.

Many of our products at Habitat were sourced abroad, and a considerable number came from India. What we were able to do was work with manufacturers and makers to improve colours and designs so that they would sell in a Western market.

After launching your first Habitat, Denise Fayolle asked you in the 1960s to design the first furniture catalogue for Prisunic. Today you are beginning to design again for Monoprix Prisunic. Would you start a new catalogue for mass production again?

MAÏMÉ ARNODIN

I have always enjoyed the challenge of selling intelligently designed products to the mass market. What Denise Fayolle achieved in the 1960s at Prisunic was a wake-up call to the whole retail industry. For far too short a time, Prisunic was demonstrating that style, design, colour and *joie de vivre* could be successfully offered and sold to the mass market and I was delighted to be a part of that exciting revolution.

After seeing what we were doing at Habitat, Denise asked us to produce a range of products for Prisunic's first mail-order catalogue in 1968; at that time, Prisunic was only selling furniture through its catalogue. The products, designed by our Design Group, were extremely well received by the French press and we produced a second range for the 1969 catalogue. Prisunic's furniture buyer, Francis Bruguière, wanted to go a step further and open up a chain of furniture stores.

That initiative and Denise's revolution, however, were killed by internal politics, which are all too prevalent in large retail organizations, and by the fact that Denise's passion and

*Early Conran KD or flat-pack furniture: simple design,
well made and easy to assemble.*

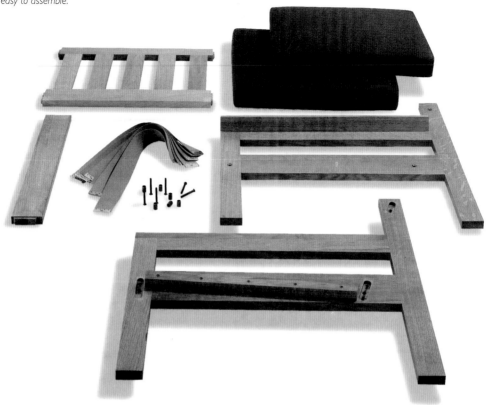

determination were misunderstood as arrogance. Eventually Francis Bruguière and three other Prisunic buyers came to work for us when we opened Habitat in France. While I am happy to be working again for Monoprix Prisunic, sadly I cannot detect the revolutionary fervour for change that existed in the 1960s.

Habitat had the qualities and values to become a worldwide business. Why did it never happen?

VITTORIO RADICE

That degree of expansion depends on many factors, but crucially on getting the right amount of investment and on timing. In Habitat's very early days, the bankers could not understand that it was not a fashion business that would be here today and gone tomorrow. It was

Our second Habitat store in Tottenham Court Road, London opened in 1965. Our advertising read 'Heel over to Habitat', which led Peace News *to comment that war had broken out in Tottenham Court Road – the long-established furniture shop Heal's, which was a near neighbour, was not too pleased by our pun.*

constantly referred to as a 'trendy' business. Because the moneymen had no sympathy for what Habitat offered, they were only prepared to lend for its development in a very cautious way.

The result was that our first expansion was very limited. By 1968 we had just five shops in total and only one, in Manchester, which was a significant distance from London. Each time we opened a new store, it cost us about £30,000, which was not an insignificant sum in those days. All the profits we made in the shops were ploughed into expansion and sometimes we had to move money around between the other businesses as well, such as the Design Group, which was the most profitable part of our enterprises, in order to maintain cash flow.

Despite this, I was determined to expand Habitat further; the business was at the stage where it needed that kind of momentum. The difficulty of securing investment tempted me into bed with Ryman's in 1968, merging our manufacturing, design and embryo Habitat businesses with Ryman's office equipment company. I became joint chairman of the new public company, Ryman Conran, with the charming Desmond Ryman.

All went well for a time, but it soon became clear that the Ryman side of the business was dedicated to using all available funds to expand, at the expense of my plans for Habitat. Ryman office shops were opening left, right and centre, all designed by my Design Group, whereas we were only able to open one new store, in Brighton, in 1969. I think the final straw was when Desmond publicly described Habitat as 'Terence's house decorating boutiques'.

Eventually, after a certain amount of anguish and recrimination, it was agreed that I should buy Habitat out of Ryman Conran. It took a certain amount of time for me to raise the finance, but the demerger was finally effected at the beginning of 1971. Most of my original staff came with me, but to my lasting sadness I had to leave behind the fabric company, contract showroom, Design Group and furniture business, which meant abandoning my factory in Thetford. Rodney Fitch, who had taken over as head of the Design Group, stayed with Ryman; later, when he managed to buy the Design Group out, it became Fitch & Co and operated out of our old offices in Hanway Place. I established a new design team, Conran Associates, with Oliver Gregory in charge, and we moved to Neal Street, Covent Garden, setting up offices in a converted banana warehouse.

After the demerger, Habitat was in a rather demoralized state. I believed that it was important to resume expansion to get the company moving again. The acquisition of Ryman's by The Burton Group proved to be the silver lining in this particular cloud. My shares soared in value and provided the funds to expand Habitat in the 1970s.

The following years were a frenzy of activity. In 1971–2 we opened seven new stores, five more in 1973, and launched the first Conran Shop. By 1974 the turnover of the business was £11 million, up £8 million in three years. A decade after I bought Habitat back from Ryman, we had forty-seven stores in all, including shops in France, Belgium and the United States.

Our first venture out of the UK was Habitat in France. In 1973, under the direction of Michael Likierman, we started with quite an ambitious programme – three stores altogether, in Montparnasse, Paris, Montpellier and a large out-of-town store and warehouse at Orgeval on the outskirts of Paris. We had borrowed heavily for this expansion.

Unfortunately, the week after we opened our first store in Montparnasse, the Arab–Israeli war started. Retail sales throughout France collapsed, we missed our sales budgets by miles and started to run out of money. Our bankers became very agitated, called me in and instructed me to stop the bleeding in France. This required the application of quite a tight tourniquet. One of the French shops was shut, staff numbers were reduced and 'frills' such as advertising and promotions were cut. Any investment that was made was strictly for immediate results, not future development. Despite this unpropitious beginning, Habitat in France did recover, and eventually we established about thirty-five stores across the country.

The year 1977 saw us breaking into the American market. We had to approach a Dutch bank to get funds to expand in the United States, because no British bank was prepared to consider the investment. Our first site was the magnificent Citicorp building in Manhattan.

The chicken brick, subject of quite a few jokes, is actually a very good way of duplicating poulet en vessie, with terracotta replacing the pig's bladder. Despite our instruction sheet, people kept cleaning the bricks with washing-up liquid, which was absorbed by the clay and then flavoured the chicken the next time the brick was used.

Chicken roasted with herbs

3 lb chicken
Salt and pepper
A little olive oil
1 clove of garlic
Thyme, basil, origano, tarragon or rosemary
– use fresh herbs if possible. Don't mix
herbs together, you get a better flavour
using them on their own.

Prepare the brick. Wipe the chicken if
frozen and place one or two sprigs of the
herb you have chosen inside. If you are
using dried herbs, you need about one
teaspoonful inside the bird and a little
more to sprinkle over the outside. It is
important to remember that rosemary and
thyme have a stronger flavour than most
other herbs, so use sparingly. Season
inside the chicken with salt and pepper
and garlic. Brush the outside with oil,
and season . Place in the brick and
cook for 1½ hours.

Roast chicken in the brick

3 lb chicken
Salt and pepper. A little olive oil
Fresh parsley. 1 clove of garlic (optional)

Prepare the brick. Wipe the chicken if
frozen. Fill the chicken with 2 or 3 large
sprigs of parsley, garlic, salt and pepper.
Brush the outside of the bird with oil
and sprinkle with a little more salt and
pepper, Put in the brick and cook for 1½ hours.

Roast chicken with lemon and mushrooms

3 lb chicken with its liver
2 large sprigs of parsley. 1 clove garlic
4 or 5 medium sized mushrooms. Olive oil
Fresh or dried basil or oregano. ½ lemon

Prepare the brick. Wipe the chicken if
frozen. Fill the chicken with the lemon
parsley, garlic, mushrooms quartered and
seasoned with salt and pepper and lastly
the liver oiled seasoned with salt and
pepper and sprinkled with herbs, brush the
outside of the chicken with oil, season
with salt and pepper and sprinkle with
herbs. Place the stuffed chicken in the
brick and cook for 1½ hours.

Roast pork with lemon and rosemary

3 lb pork loin
2 inches lemon rind
2 cloves of garlic
Olive oil
Rosemary
Salt and pepper

Prepare the brick. Wipe the meat and make
some small incisions through the skin
with a sharp knife. Insert a small piece
of lemon rind and a small piece of garlic
into each. Brush the meat with oil and
season with salt, pepper and sprinkle
with a desertspoonful of dried rosemary
or a twig of fresh rosemary in the brick
with the meat. Cook in the usual way for
1½ hours. You will need to pour off the
excess fat before making a sauce or
gravy from the juices in the bottom of
the brick. Serve the pork with baked or
puréed potatoes or a dish of haricot
, or butter beans.

Chicken brick instructions

Soak the whole brick in cold water for about 10 minutes then give it a good scrub before using for the first time. Do not use detergent, the taste stays in the clay. It improves the flavour of the food, without over-powering it, to rub the inside of the brick with a clove of garlic each time. No fats need be added apart from brushing the meat with a little olive oil before season-ing. The brick should always be put in a cold oven set at a very high temp-erature, 250C, 500F, gas mark 9. Cooking time is 1½ hrs for meat, or birds, weighing 3 lbs. The meat does not need to be basted during cooking, it browns mir-aculously inside the brick. The juice ob-tained can be made into a sauce to go with the meat or just strained and served. Chickens or pieces of meat up to 3lbs fit in the brick and it is best to fill the brick well. For frozen meat thaw and wipe before cooking. To clean the brick, scrub well in plenty of hot water with 2 tablespoons of vinegar or salt.

HABITAT CHICKEN BRICK

Ham roasted in the brick

3 lb piece of ham
2 onions 2 carrots 4 allspice
6 peppercorns 2 celery stalks
For the crust:
1 breakfastcup of fresh breadcrumbs ·
4 oz soft brown sugar
1 desertspoonful mild mustard
A little fruit juice or cider for mixing

Soak the ham for 8 hours. Put it in a
pan with the carrots, onion, celery,
peppercorns, allspice. Bring gently to
the boil and simmer for 45 minutes.
Meanwhile prepare the brick and make the
mixture for the crust. Mix the
breadcrumbs and mustard with enough
fruit juice or cider to make a paste.
Peel the ham and spike the fat with about
12 cloves. Spread over the breadcrumb
mixture, place in the brick and roast for
1½ hours. Quite a lot of fat comes out of the
meat so it's best to pour it off before
using the juice to serve with meat. Add
a little more fruit juice or cider to the
juices in the brick. Fruit can be added
to this — stewed, fresh, or dried apricots
cranberries or apples.

Pigeons roasted in the brick

4-6 young pigeons
1 rasher of streaky bacon for each bird
Dried thyme or 2 large branches of thyme
A little olive oil
Salt and pepper
1 clove of garlic

Prepare the brick. Wipe the pigeons with
a cloth and brush with the oil. Season
with salt and pepper, bearing in mind
that the bacon may be salty. Wrap each
bird in a piece of the bacon and put them
in the brick with the thyme and cook for
1½ hours. Pigeons cooked this way are
good served with boiled rice, risotto or
purée sauce — something to absorb
their delicious sauce — and perhaps
a salad, watercress or chicory.

Mixed roast meats in the brick

1 piece of pork tenderloin
1 piece of tame rabbit per person
1 small piece of ham, collar or gammon
enough for a slice for each person
1 rasher of streaky bacon for each piece
of rabbit
4-6 oz chicken livers
2 inch strip of lemon peel
2 cloves of garlic
Oregano or thyme
Salt and pepper. A little olive oil

Half cook the piece of ham the day before.
Prepare the brick. Wipe the rabbit, season
with pepper, wrap each piece in a rasher
of bacon – the bacon will salt it enough.
Wipe the piece of tenderloin, make some
small incisions in it with a sharp knife
and push a small piece of lemon rind and
garlic into each. About 4 incisions is
enough to make the meat subtly lemony
oil and season with a little salt and
pepper and a little of the herbs. Wipe,
oil and season the chicken livers sprinkling
them with the herbs. Put the chicken
livers in the brick first, then the other
meats. Put the brick in the oven and
cook for 1½ hours.

LEFT: *A rather dodgy bunch! Phillip Pollock, Michael Likierman, T Conran and Oliver Gregory at the opening of Habitat in France.*

BELOW: *Habitat, Montparnasse, the first shop in France, September 1973.*

Because of a slump in the New York property market and the fact that Citicorp was the only new building being erected in the city at the time, we managed to obtain very favourable terms, a rental of $10 per square foot fixed for twenty years. Habitat – or Conran's as it had to be called in the States due to copyright problems – grew to about fifteen stores over the next decade, mainly along the east coast, including a shop located in a wonderful old tobacco warehouse in Georgetown.

At the peak of Habitat's expansion, there were about forty stores in the UK, added to the thirty-five in France and fifteen in the United States. But our difficulties with investment never really went away. In today's climate, now that Gap and IKEA have proved to be successful around the world, I'm sure that Habitat would have found it easier to get international funding.

Aside from investment – and those sudden blips of timing – there was another problem that I faced in my attempt to develop a truly international business; and it was a problem that you also saw during your own time at Habitat. This was the fact that many of our colleagues, especially the French, were convinced that each country needed its own infrastructure and that what sold well in the UK would not necessarily sell in France or America. Of course, a certain amount of fine tuning is necessary in any retail enterprise that has multiple international branches, but not so that it makes it impossible to have a central resource of buying and design, with all the economic advantages that this brings with it.

Do you believe in 'give and take'?

GEORGIA GLYNN SMITH

Give and take is essentially the art of compromise. But it is always a struggle for people with deeply held beliefs to decide how far they will compromise to preserve or create a relationship, whether at a personal, team or client level. Seeing the other person's point of view can be simple common sense, but it can also lead to a solution that satisfies neither side and results in the loss of clarity of vision.

I well remember a market research report that was prepared for Habitat in 1978. In those days, before the proliferation of focus groups canvassing opinions in every area of life, market research was not easily dismissed. The report prepared for Habitat appeared to demonstrate quite clearly that our products were almost universally disliked. Habitat was characterized as cold, hard and clinical; the Laura Ashley style was seen as the customer's dream. The message of the report was that Habitat could not expand successfully unless we followed a more conservative path.

While I knew that Habitat's design philosophy was right – although I was aware that the quality of our products was quite often not up to standard – the report really rocked the boat with our buyers and management team, as it seemed to call into question the very

principles of the business. It even shook my conviction about the direction we were taking. What I didn't realize at the time was that we were creating a style that would gradually gain more acceptance.

This report had far-reaching consequences. It turned Habitat into something of a talking shop. Nobody felt we had a clear direction any longer. The buyers tried to react to the report's findings by sourcing products that somehow answered the findings of the research. I tried to steer the company back to what I believed, in my gut, that it should be. The business as a whole undoubtedly suffered a loss of direction and the compromises we all made in the process seem to me to highlight the risks associated with too much give and take.

You are invited to a party to celebrate the opening of

conran's

The first of our American home furnishings stores
Monday October 3, 1977 5-8 pm
The Market at Citicorp Center 54th Street and Third Avenue
Please bring this invitation

Conran's, The Market at Citicorp Center, 160 East 54th Street, New York 10022 (212) 371-2225

A stylish but perhaps slightly insensitive opening invitation to our first New York store.
The name 'Habitat' was already registered in the United States, so we had to call the
store 'Conran's' — or pay the $3 million asking price for the right to use the name.

Was your interest in design motivated by a desire for commercial success or by your belief that you could change the way this generation thinks about their surroundings?
RUPERT HAMBRO

I've always tried to make products that represent good value for money. In the beginning it was very difficult because I only had a tiny audience and could only make things in very small quantities. I more or less succeeded in my aim when I expanded Habitat around the world, but when I consider the impact of IKEA today, I have to admit I only scratched the surface.

Although I certainly realized quite early on that unless I made money I was unlikely to remain in business, I have never been been solely motivated by profit. On the occasions when I have made compromises for profitable reasons, I have always regretted them and they have proved in the long term not to be the right direction for the company.

The success of the entrepreneurial spirit relies on an innate sense of timing and judgement. However, these factors must be informed by various external triggers. Have you always managed to match your instinct to market needs? Can you identify the most successful example, and one that missed the mark?
DAVID CHALONER

In 1974, during the recession caused by the three-day week, it became desperately important to do something about sagging sales at Habitat. I came up with the idea of Habitat Basics: a collection of one hundred home furnishing products at remarkably low prices. We put the range together and promoted it with simple black and white illustrations, printed in the form of a tabloid newspaper. Basics did wonders for our sales, but devastated our profit margins!

Much later, in 1982, we revisited the Basics idea. Around the same time, we franchised Habitat to Seibu in Japan. The Japanese thought Basics was a wonderful idea and asked if they could open independent shops under that name. Stupidly, we agreed. The shops were subsequently developed under a 'no name, no brand' byline. They are now called Muji. I wish they were still mine!

In my Habitat–Mothercare days, we started two new clothing brands. One of them was called 'NOW' and was for teenagers; the other was called 'Anonymous' and was designed for twenty-somethings. Both brands suffered from bad buying and lack of conviction on the part of the management team. I failed to convince them that they potentially had a hot property on their hands.

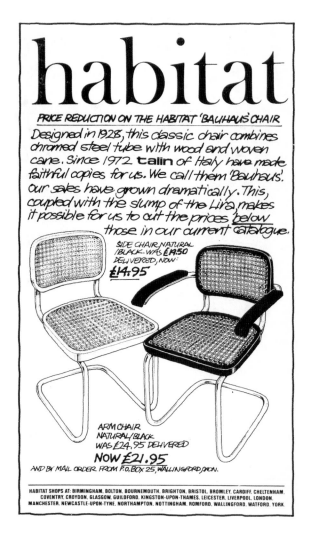

Simple product advertising that ran next to The Times *diary page.*
The approach was suggested to me by Jeremy Bulmore, creative director
of J Walter Thompson.

What has been your biggest disappointment?

ILSE CRAWFORD

The fact that I no longer run Habitat. I regret having to give it up as one of the prices I paid
to extricate myself from Storehouse.

Vittorio Radice and I celebrate Habitat's thirtieth anniversary at the refitted King's Road store.

Shopfronts and catalogues provided the means to showcase our products. The first Habitat catalogue, which came out in 1965, simply consisted of loose sheets, attached in one corner; eventually the catalogue grew to eighty-eight pages, all in full colour, with a special department within the company dedicated to its production.

If you had continued to develop Habitat as a private company and still owned it, what would Habitat look like today?
CLIFF BURROWS

Habitat would probably look a lot more like The Conran Shop, but with the lower prices that can be achieved by a very much larger retailer's buying power. There would also be a 'basics' collection that would run right the way through every merchandise category, would offer the very best design and best value for money, and that would put Muji out of business.

I've always seen Habitat as occupying an important gap between IKEA and The Conran Shop and Heal's: IKEA as a source for people setting up home for the first time; Habitat for those settling down and keen to do up their home properly; The Conran Shop and Heal's for those who have reached a stage in life where they can start exploring different directions. Obviously, with IKEA's expansion into the UK, Habitat has to distance itself from them; there's no reason to emulate IKEA (particularly as they are both owned by Ingvar Kamprad). But I don't think Habitat is really exploiting the gap that exists. It seems to have become IKEA's styling shop; the ideas Habitat comes up with seem to be quickly knocked off and offered at a cheaper price in IKEA. Tom Dixon, who is Habitat's design director, is an incredibly talented designer, but I don't think he is a retailer at heart. Judging from Habitat's recent revival of 1960s and '70s products and its *Wallpaper*-esque catalogue, his sights seem to be set on impressing the design community rather than giving consumers what they might want. I think it would be better to concentrate on investing in the best of today's creative talent and then promoting the results in a way that ordinary people can understand.

You are a genius with all your bright ideas and sense for good design but when shall you learn to take care of what you already have and not only put new activities on your desk? Not too late, I hope. (I had to learn the same lesson a long time ago.)
INGVAR KAMPRAD

Although I have a tremendous admiration for you and what you have achieved with IKEA, I am a very different person with very different ambitions and interests. I've been called a hedonist by some of my friends. You on the other hand are the least hedonistic person I've ever met – you relish austerity. In fact, you relish it so much I can only believe that, as one of the richest and brightest people in the world, austerity has become your hedonism.

I enormously enjoy the diversity of my life. Maybe I'm a jack of all trades and master of none, but if a new and relevant challenge came along, I'd probably leap at it.

Running the biggest, most successful and most profitable home furnishing business in the world is obviously quite enough for you. As you believe that you can only do one thing properly, perhaps you'd like me to run Habitat again?

STOREHOUSE TO BUTLERS WHARF

In autumn 1981, Habitat became a public company. Soon after, we took over Mothercare; eighteen months of hard work went into transforming its image, products and stores. Then, in 1983, we bought Heal's, a sadly down-at-heel furniture company established in the early nineteenth century, but which had acquired a reputation for making and selling good modern design under the direction of Ambrose Heal, the grandson of the founder. By this stage, the annual turnover of the group was £380 million.

The Heal's building in Tottenham Court Road became the new headquarters for Habitat–Mothercare. We converted the building, moved a branch of Habitat into part of it and opened a branch of Mothercare in another, as well as retaining a sizable portion for Heal's itself. The group offices, photographic studios, catalogue and advertising production departments and archive occupied the upper floors.

In 1986 came the biggest step of all, when Habitat–Mothercare merged with British Home Stores. The new company, which we named Storehouse, had a turnover well in excess of £1 billion. With outlets in every high street now under our control, the merger seemed to offer a real opportunity to introduce intelligently designed products to the mass market. Sadly, several years of acrimony and frustration later, that particular dream came to an end.

The Storehouse years coincided with another ambitious scheme, to develop Butlers Wharf, a derelict Docklands area, into a thriving mixed-use community. In the event, this huge project also failed to go according to plan. We managed to create the Design Museum and its resident restaurant, the Blue Print Café, and to convert some of the warehouses into residential use before the recession set in and scuppered the development for several years.

In running a public business, is it possible to combine excellent taste with providing adequate returns to shareholders?

MICHAEL STODDART

If the idea is good, the business is well run and well financed and the product is demonstrably good value for money, I firmly believe that intelligent design can provide more than adequate returns to shareholders. You and I were both involved with Hepworth's, a public company, when we started Next in 1982. At that time the concept of the shops, their design and the products we offered were very different to anything else on the high street. Perhaps not excellent taste, but pretty good nevertheless.

I remember when we came up with the name Next. The Hepworth directors in Leeds hated it and commissioned some market research that, surprise, surprise, confirmed their view. The conclusion was that the name would be a terrible hindrance to the business. The creative directors in London, on the other hand, loved the concept. *Their* research showed that it was a wonderful name. I think the lesson to be learned is that research is primarily historic rather than predictive; it can only tell you what people like, not what they *might* like. To determine what customers might like means going on gut instinct and, to a large extent, this is always a subjective view. My idea of taste may differ from yours; it's a pretty difficult concept to define. Taste and style are movable feasts and all the more fascinating for it.

You developed a successful business with Habitat, then were basically a failure as chairman of Next. You have since been successful again with the development of the restaurant chain. Why the difference in performance between the successful and unsuccessful ventures?

ROCCO FORTE

You've got it wrong again! I was chairman of Hepworth's menswear when we decided to buy a chain of eighty rainwear shops and turn them into outlets for womenswear. The chain became Next; our design group thought of the name, designed the interiors and set a style for the merchandise. Trevor Morgan was the managing director and George Davies and his then wife, Liz, joined the team as merchandise director and designer. George was not the founder of Next, although he made a great contribution to its initial success, as did Trevor.

Well after the hugely successful launch, I resigned as chairman and George succeeded Trevor as managing director. I resigned because Habitat–Mothercare, which I also chaired, had just acquired Richard Shops, which was something of a high-street competitor to Next. I felt that being chairman of both companies could be seen by our shareholders as a conflict of interests. As it happens, some of the directors and shareholders of Next wanted Habitat–Mothercare to acquire them; we should have done so.

To answer your question, I think the difference in performance between successful and unsuccessful ventures is down to positive leadership conveying a clear message to all the staff. I'm sure your new hotel group will succeed because it has your passion and direction behind it. I'm also sure that George will do wonders for M & S, as merchandising is definitely the message that its customers need to hear, rather than disorganized titivation.

Around the time of Storehouse, you once told me that you would like to become the 'King of the High Street'. Do you feel that you have achieved that ambition, although in another field, or is there still room for improvement?

ANTONIO CARLUCCIO

I cannot imagine that I could ever have said that I wanted to be King of the High Street, even in my sillier moments. I certainly hoped that I could demonstrate through Mothercare, Habitat and BhS that the public would like and buy well-designed products if they were offered to them at affordable prices.

Would the Conran story – and the shape of the high street – be very different if you had paid a bit more and taken over British Home Stores rather than done a merger?

PATIENCE WHEATCROFT

Yes, I believe it would have made a terrific difference. But at that time, it was either merge or go away. Sadly, we didn't go away and the result was Storehouse, the huge company created by the merger of the Habitat–Mothercare group – which also included Richards, Heal's, Conran Associates, The Conran Shop and part of FNAC – with British Home Stores, a rather downmarket chain selling clothing and homeware with outlets in practically every high street. With hindsight, we should not have agreed to a fifty-fifty deal as it caused a political log jam.

The difference that an outright takeover would have made can be clearly demonstrated when you consider our previous experience with Mothercare, a company started in the 1960s by Selim Zilkha and Jimmy Goldsmith, who had cannily identified a gap in the market for products designed for pregnant women, babies and children. I got to know Selim quite well later on, when I was expanding Habitat. He was a charming man, always exquisitely dressed and a genius when it came to business systems and cost control. Every day he'd leave his grand apartment in Langham Place, get into his chauffeured Rolls, spread a nappy over his Savile Row suit and read the papers while he was driven to the Mothercare head office in Watford, a clapped-out old sweet factory with holes in the carpet and battered desks.

Selim ran the tightest ship one could possibly imagine and knew down to the last farthing what each store was costing him per square foot. It was around the time that computerized systems, such as EPOS, were beginning to be used in retailing and Selim had set up his own systems to provide detailed information on every aspect of his business. I'd met him socially and expressed an interest in getting to know more about the way these systems worked, as I was keen to introduce them myself.

Although Mothercare had done very well as a public company, in the late 1970s it began to attract a lot of criticism and sales started to suffer. It was obvious that what was missing was decent merchandise. Selim was fixated on cutting costs and was always trying to get his buyers to source things more cheaply. The stores and the products were really grim, in nasty colours like avocado, burnt orange and cream. Before Habitat had become a public company, Selim had tried to buy it, recognizing that we had got the right approach to merchandise. When Mothercare began to attract criticism and Selim found himself increasingly attracted to life in America, he came to us and suggested that we might like to buy Mothercare instead. After some amicable – and heated – discussions, the Habitat–Mothercare group was formed in 1981. At that time Mothercare consisted of over four hundred shops and operated in ten countries.

In many ways, Mothercare was like a blank slate and provided a crash course on how to reposition a company. We changed everything, from the logo and the interiors of the stores to the products on sale. The shops, which had been quite clinical in appearance, were redesigned to be gentler and more charming, using 'sweet pea' colours, which also defined the look of some of the products, the graphics, the catalogue and the packaging. Although many of the products, such as buggies and prams, could not be changed overnight, we were able to introduce enough new merchandise to present the new-look shops to the press eighteen months after the takeover. It all worked dramatically well and what had become a steep decline in sales turned into fairly rapid growth.

At the time of the merger with British Home Stores, we were quite convinced that we could effect a similar revitalization at BhS, as we renamed it. What we forgot was that our acquisition of Mothercare had been a takeover and that most of the people there, including many of the buyers and senior executives, had shared our view that change was necessary and were equally anxious to see the product range improved.

We all started out with the best intentions and things went well for a while. We set up an independent design group to work on all aspects of repositioning BhS. But quite soon political rifts developed. The senior management at BhS were not entirely convinced by our proposals and 'us' quickly became 'us' and 'them'. We believed that the right direction was for BhS to adopt a similar philosophy to Gap, which had not yet expanded to the UK. It soon became apparent that the BhS buyers wanted to pick and choose and did not want to follow the design group's overall direction. The buyers found it difficult to accept that more sophisticated designs could ever generate the kind of turnover generated by ten million dozen pale pink polyester cardis.

The purpose of this advertising was to demonstrate that things were changing at BhS as they had changed at Mothercare.

We started a company called 'Storecard' that provided plastic for all Storehouse companies.

Many discussions ensued and quite a few arguments. As this was a merger and because the board was evenly balanced between BhS and Habitat–Mothercare, nothing was ever properly resolved. It was obvious that change was going to be slow and painful. Everything became a compromise; politics reigned supreme.

The press, of course, picked up on this. A journalist on the *Sunday Express* reported that things were not going well on the board, that there was friction between the two sides of the company and speculated whether there might be a takeover in the offing. Before long, Storehouse was inundated with takeover rumours and bids. It was at that point in the late 1980s when people believed that money grew on trees, so there were plenty of people prepared to invest in such schemes.

Our first hostile approach came when Tony Clegg of Mountleigh got the finance together to make a bid; the idea was to break up the group and sell off the parts individually. He asked me to sell him my shares, but I wouldn't: I believed that we were just beginning to turn round BhS and as chairman I was in it for the opportunity to make profitable change rather than the chance to make a personal fortune. Furthermore, the whole group was making a £125 million profit at that time and our merchant banks advised us not to accept the offer. No sooner had the Mountleigh bid failed, than Benlox, who took the same view about breaking up the group, made a bid. Finally, it was Edelman: altogether three different bids in six months. I spent most of my time visiting banks and financial institutions, talking to spotty City analysts and the press, trying to defend the company from the vultures. It was a nightmare.

My simple idea of how we could improve the design and quality of what BhS offered on the high street got completely submerged by the politics and intrigue of an embattled public company. I tried to be a benevolent autocratic chairman, but eventually I was outmanoeuvred in my ambitions, which is why I gradually withdrew to try to do something more interesting with my life. I do believe that if Storehouse had been successful, the shape of the high street would be different now. It was a waste of a wonderful opportunity that I regret to this day.

Michael Julien and you appeared to have very complementary skills. What happened?

ROGER SEELIG

Michael Julien was, and is, a very nice man. He came with excellent references and was financially astute. He had been the finance director of BICC, Guinness and Midland Bank, but he wanted to be a chief executive and this was the job I offered him, imagining that he would be happy to leave the creative decisions to me. With hindsight, I'm quite sure that if I had remained chief executive and he had been finance director, things would have worked out well.

As it was, Michael clearly wanted to make Storehouse his own company – and I can't blame him for that. But instead of providing clear leadership, he started canvassing the opinions of practically everyone within the company, all of whom were jostling for position. I felt increasingly sidelined. Beware of chief executives who immediately hire expensive consultants when they join a company, as this signals their lack of confidence in their own judgement.

With Michael Julien, whom I appointed chief executive of Storehouse in February 1988.

What did you learn about the joys and sorrows of corporate life during your time as chairman of Storehouse? With the benefit of hindsight, did the concept of Storehouse as a group make sense? And is it possible to introduce design ideas like yours into an old-fashioned and established group like BhS – or are the two completely incompatible?

CHRISTOPHER BLAND

The joys and sorrows of corporate life that I experienced at Storehouse (where you were a non-executive director) probably echo elements of your own experiences as chairman of the BBC and now of British Telecom. Making a success of corporate life mainly depends on having the right people around you and working as a dedicated team, trying to change the things that need to change.

Sadly, during my years at Storehouse we were never able to build that dedicated team who shared a simple vision and determination to succeed. Too many people were pulling in opposite directions and too many consultants were rowing their own very expensive boats. I still believe that if we had had a strong chief executive, who shared my vision for the revitalization of BhS, Storehouse could have become a success, the UK's answer to Gap.

You ask if Storehouse as a group made sense. I believe it did. Many of the companies in the group were fundamentally compatible. Mothercare and BhS shared a similar market – babies and pregnant mums in the case of Mothercare, and women and children in the case of BhS. Richards related to BhS womenswear. Habitat and FNAC related to the homeware side of BhS and could have pulled together most successfully as a single home entertainment and furnishing emporium.

As far as introducing new ideas into established companies is concerned, I believe that you can only effect change by being brave. Gap has had an impact that no one could have predicted, even with the use of the most sophisticated market research. If you look at the way that supermarkets such as Sainsbury's and Tesco have developed in this country over the last fifteen years it is obvious that really massive changes can take place in old and established companies if the philosophy and will is there.

With regard to Storehouse, what is your opinion of the City after expelling you from the company you created and would you ever consider going public again?

RODNEY KINSMAN

I was never expelled from Storehouse by anybody but myself. I made a decision that there were better things to do in life and withdrew over a two-year period, first as chief executive, then as executive chairman and finally as a non-executive director. I left Storehouse in 1990. I don't expect or want to be involved in running a public company again.

Looking back at your involvement with BhS and Storehouse, do you regret your involvement and what are the lessons you have learned?

PETER DAVIS

No, I don't regret it, although I probably could have spent the three or four years I had at Storehouse more constructively. I fervently wish that I could have had you to work with as chief executive of the group but as we both know that was politically impossible at the time. As a team I'm sure we would have worked very well together.

What did I learn?

I learned that mergers don't work, that takeover attempts can be demoralizing to the target business – especially three in a row. That City analysts on the whole have all the consistency of the Vicar of Bray, that bankers and institutional investors are fair-weather friends. That much of the energies of a public company are diverted into dealing with shareholders, that newspaper journalists can be vultures and troublemakers.

But I also learned that you can achieve things quickly as a public company and that the change that occurred in retailing in the 1980s could not have been achieved by a private company. I also learned a great deal from going round our jointly owned Savacentre stores with John and David Sainsbury.

And, finally, I learned that politics in business is immensely destructive.

When you left Storehouse and we bought back The Conran Shop and the rights to use your name, it was finally the end of an incredible story. How did you feel?

BOB WIGLEY

First of all, exhausted; secondly, disappointed. As one of the team of bankers who helped to build Storehouse, I expect you shared some of my disappointment that the grand plan didn't work out as we had hoped. For me, the disappointment was offset by relief – relief to be the master of my own destiny again, to (almost) get my name back and to have my beloved Conran Shop back under my control. For this I had to sacrifice Habitat and the right to trade under any name that bracketed the words 'Conran' and 'design', which is why my design group today has to be called Conran & Partners. But as it turned out, this was only the start of a new and much more rewarding story for me.

You said at the time that the day we opened in the Michelin Building was the happiest day of your life. How important to you was the opening of The Conran Shop and Bibendum?

GEOFF MARSHALL

The Conran Shop was initially born out of my frustration at having to reject products because they were too expensive or perceived as too unusual for Habitat's customers. We opened the first shop in 1973 on the Fulham Road site of the first Habitat, which moved to a new location in the King's Road. Maggie Heaney was our first buyer; in 1978 my sister Priscilla moved back to Britain from France and took over the role. We were able to sell not only the work of well-known designers but also to encourage new design talent and young craftsmen, simply because we could afford to commission in relatively small quantities. In some ways, The Conran Shop became an experimental arm of Habitat; if a product worked in The Conran Shop and was cheap enough, we could introduce it to the mass market via Habitat.

Over the years I had grown to love and admire the delightfully quirky Art Deco architecture of the Michelin Building, across the road from our shop, and I couldn't believe my luck when Paul Hamlyn and I managed to buy it in 1985. For the next two years, we all worked incredibly hard to restore the building and convert it to provide space for a new Conran Shop, publishing offices and a restaurant; the project provided me with a great deal of creative satisfaction at a time when I was just beginning to become enmeshed in the complexities of corporate life at Storehouse. The day the Michelin Building reopened was indeed one of the very happiest of my professional career; it was wonderful to see it flooded with life.

The new Conran Shop was three times the size of the first one, and Priscilla and the team did a marvellous job helping to stock it with products that, although sourced from the four corners of the globe, had the same consistency that had been such a feature of Habitat in its early days. Today, we have expanded in a modest way, opening new branches in Marylebone, in the old Eiffel building in the rue du Bac in Paris, in Shinjuku Park Tower, Tokyo and within my Bridgemarket development in New York. It's a considerable consolation for the loss of Habitat.

Detail of the beautiful and outrageous Art Deco façade of the Michelin Building, Fulham Road, London, showing one of the stained glass windows we reinstated after the originals had vanished.

The Marylebone Conran Shop, together with Orrery restaurant on the first floor, has been a most successful development by our architects.

In the days when you were one of the largest retailers in this country, with BhS, Habitat, Heal's and Mothercare, you believed that there was no conflict between design excellence and the mass market. I wonder if now that those days are over and you run your own exclusive Conran Shops, you have changed your mind about this matter?

DAVID QUEENSBERRY

All of us who have worked in the mass market know that to be successful there is inevitably an element of compromise involved, usually to do with price and quality. At the same time, as our ceramic designs with Midwinter demonstrated back in the 1950s, it has always been possible to sell good quality contemporary products to the mass market provided the price is right. I remember buying one of the designs you produced for Crown Staffordshire, a dark green tea set, and giving it to my parents as a Christmas present; it became one of their treasured possessions.

I found and still do find that the mass market offers a greater and more worthwhile challenge than the more exclusive shops and restaurants with which I am now mainly involved. Retailers in the mass market have for years had a cynical attitude to their customers' taste. The struggle to offer products of more integrity that are also appropriate to the world we live in today seems to me to be both worthwhile and rewarding.

When you look at the high street today, you can certainly see an improvement in the general taste level, especially when you look at the design of some mass-market clothing, IKEA products, small cars, most electronic equipment and most definitely in the case of food retailers like Sainsbury's, Tesco, Waitrose and the excellent presentation and packaging of Boots. But then go into your average out-of-town furniture retailer and the products seem almost as ghastly as they always were.

Our company still works for some mass-market retailers such as Monoprix Prisunic in France, Vision Express UK, and a new Japanese clothing company that is going to be a big challenge to Gap. We also design a large number of products that reach the mass market, either directly or by percolating downwards from our more elitist Conran Shops and restaurants. That's one definite change I can detect; in the past, the mass market was barely affected by what was going on at the top end and there was much more polarity in terms of taste; today there isn't.

Where do you see the future of middle-market British retailing when so many of the great brands built in the second half of the twentieth century appear to be in decline?

ALAN K P SMITH

Like any business, retailing needs an idea and a philosophy behind it and a strong figurehead at the helm. This philosophy can be passed down from generation to generation as it was at

Marks & Spencer when you were there, or it can be dissipated as in the case of Sears, Mothercare, Montgomery Ward and sadly also now M & S.

When a retailer loses its identity and becomes so huge and rudderless, the only option seems to be to offer goods at a discount, which usually means erosion of margins and eventual decline, inevitably leading to chapter eleven or bankruptcy when the next recession comes along.

There are a few cheerful stories of companies such as Gap and Selfridges that have been able to reinvent themselves; I very much hope that Mothercare, which has been so grossly abused over recent years, will with your sensitive fathering be able to recover its ethical position. The brand is still just alive – give it the oxygen it so desperately needs!

You have had a very varied experience with finance people! As a creative entrepreneur, what advice do you have for finance people on how to work with people like you, not just in the sense of being effective, but also in terms of making up for your weaknesses and lack of interest in the area?
LANCE MOIR

I suppose my apparent disdain for many finance people has arisen out of their lack of interest in the products we designed and sold, and the service we gave. I am extremely sensitive to issues of cost – both the costs associated with running a business and the cost of the products we offer for sale. But I strongly dislike the 'bottom-line' mentality, especially when it is applied indiscriminately, as if it were a good or prudent thing in itself. One perhaps rather trivial example that springs to mind concerns the production of Conran Shop carrier bags. Over the years I have fought many battles with accountants who have periodically wanted to save money by making the bags out of plastic rather than good quality paper. I strongly believe that to do so would undermine the ethos and message of the shop.

Although financial results are not the most important thing for me, daily, weekly and monthly sales and margin reports can be a useful source of adrenaline (equally, of course, they can be depressing). In general, it's very important to me to be able to have wide-ranging discussions with my financial colleagues about the business in general, and new projects in particular. They need to share my entrepreneurial philosophy and to understand and get excited about the whole picture, but also be ready to apply a cool damp cloth to the fevered brow on occasions. One of the reasons that I have enjoyed the last ten years of my business life so much is that I have been able to have that sort of relationship. It is something I have always looked for, but rarely found in the past.

From the time that we first met some thirty years ago, what are the most significant changes in design and appreciation of food that have taken place in this country and abroad; and how have you managed to combine a consistency of excellence with commercial success?

PETER PALUMBO

Even on the most superficial level, people's attitudes to design, food and a whole variety of what you might call 'lifestyle' issues have changed out of all recognition. In Britain, there has been a very welcome acceptance of modernity in design as we have at last begun to stop clinging to the comfort blanket of the past. In terms of food, one has only to compare the range of produce in the average supermarket today with that of thirty years ago to see that we are no longer frightened of styles of cooking from countries outside our own. It wasn't so long ago that you could only buy one variety of olive oil, and that was from a chemist; now most supermarkets stock dozens of different varieties. Today, people are better informed, through television programmes, holidays abroad, books and magazines, about other influences and other ways of living and I can only see that as something to be welcomed.

I think excellence is largely dependent on creativity. For a long time in business there has been a polarity between 'creative' people and 'finance' people. Finance people tend to be inherently conservative and often rely on research forecasts that demonstrate that the middle of the road is the most successful and profitable path to follow. But in recent years people such as James Dyson and Norman Foster have demonstrated that uncompromising creativity can go hand in hand with financial success. I think that creative people should be involved in all aspects of business, not just as consultants, but in the day-to-day running of a company and in all the decision-making processes. They are the people who really make a company a success.

When you opened your first shop in London more than thirty-five years ago, you became an icon of British culture. How has the retail industry changed over the years? How has your business had to evolve to keep pace?

TOM FORD

Retailing has changed dramatically over the past thirty-five years as retailers have realized that they can become their own brand rather than simply a space where they sell other people's brands. The department store ethos, where customers browsed among a number of different brands, has given way to a situation where the shop itself is the brand. The customer is choosing not only a product, but the whole image of the company, expressed in its graphics, the design of its interior and its packaging, as much as in the goods themselves.

The result is that retailers have to take a much greater interest in what they sell and the way they promote it because, if they don't get it right, then they damage their own reputation. This is, of course, the downside. The upside is the ability to control your suppliers, your prices, your margins and your future!

The shops that I have been involved with have always been that sort of business. Today, better information systems mean that we can provide both a better service and anticipate the needs and wants of our customers. The liberalization of world markets has also made it much easier to both source and sell, from and to a much wider audience who have begun to appreciate how contemporary design can make their lives more enjoyable.

How will environmental issues affect retailing in the twenty-first century?
DAVID KRANTZ

I am certain that environmental issues will assume an even greater importance as a larger proportion of the population becomes aware of the potentially devastating consequences of our patterns of consumption. In retailing, the great debate is between fashion and sustainability. Contemporary retailing relies heavily on fashion; fashion, in all its forms, makes the wheels of commerce spin faster and faster, which in turn generates employment, not only at home but also abroad. On the other hand, fashion also leads to conspicuously wasteful consumerism, which is certainly a contemporary evil. Where consumers have already had an impact is in the sourcing of materials. IKEA, for example, has recently guaranteed that in future all the timber they use will come from identifiably sustainable sources.

I would identify the proliferation of out-of-town stores and hypermarkets as a particular environmental problem. Such developments consume vast tracts of countryside, turn inner-city areas into commercial wastelands, and increase reliance on the car. These gigantic temples of consumerism have already caused considerable damage in the United States; here, planners are at last beginning to face up to the problem.

I would like retailers to rethink the whole issue of packaging. Look at the boxes and crates piled up at the back door of the average retailer, then look in your own bin after a visit to the supermarket, add the two together and you will realize that much of what you have paid for has been of very little use, as it does not protect or contain what you have bought. Most of all that cardboard and plastic is just sale promotion. If manufacturers and retailers had to show the price of the packaging separate to the product, it would really focus attention on the huge waste that results from over-packaging.

The constant redesign and refitting of stores is another area of needless waste. When changes happen frequently, it can be a sign that a quick fix is needed for sagging sales, or that the store environment is more important than the merchandise. I believe that if you get the store design right at the beginning and use good quality materials for surfaces and finishes that take on a pleasing patina through use, then constant change becomes unnecessary. Well-displayed merchandise should always be the message.

In a time of increased waste and consumerism, if you were able to communicate a way to reverse this trend through an act, what would it be?

JILL WEBB

I don't think a single act (apart from getting rid of George W Bush) could ever resolve the problems of waste and rampant consumerism, but companies do sit up and take notice when customers boycott their products or mount very vocal campaigns to force them to take greater environmental responsibility. Naming and shaming seems to be quite effective, particularly when it comes to multinationals. My hopes in this department lie with young educated people around the world who are increasingly forcing governments to put safeguarding the environment onto their agendas. Learning to live with fewer products, but products that are better quality and more labour-intensive to produce, would be one solution.

Sometimes, however, the public profile that companies enjoy can be a very effective means of getting an environmental message across. In the early 1980s, under the guidance of the World Wildlife Fund, Habitat sponsored the reintroduction of the Large Blue butterfly, which had died out in Britain in 1979. It was just one species among the many that have disappeared from our countryside since the war, but small gestures can help to focus people's attention on wider issues.

How did you manage to get the name Bibendum and become the owner of that mythical brand for England?

MAÏMÉ ARNODIN

Over the years I got to know quite a bit about the history of Michelin, was a great admirer of its original marketing and, of course, was a frequent user of its guides and maps. We designed a range of glasses for Habitat and I suggested we called them Bibendum, after 'Nunc est Bibendum' ('now is the time to drink'), one of Michelin's captions for an early poster, depicting Monsieur Bibendum drinking broken glass, nails and sharp flints and not getting punctured.

When I decided to include a restaurant in our development of the Michelin Building, I wanted to call it Bibendum – it seemed a natural choice given that the Art Deco stained-glass windows portraying Monsieur Bibendum are such a wonderful feature of the building's design. At this point, Michelin's lawyers became focused on the fact that they had never properly protected their Bibendum trademark. I entered into an agreement that allowed me to use the name for the restaurant and its equipment but nothing else. However, they couldn't stop a company called Bibendum Wine from using their name. Now that Monsieur Bibendum has been recognized as the number one logo in the world, they have quite rightly protected it energetically.

Why do you love 'Bibendum' so much?
PATRICK LEPERCQ

'Love' is the right word. Monsieur Bibendum stands for charm, humour and friendliness. He's a character that closely represents the product he advertises yet can adapt to any situation in any country and still remain relevant and recognizable.

Behind Monsieur Bibendum lies the most brilliant marketing campaign that any company has ever devised. The foresight of the Michelin brothers, when it came to envisaging the future of motoring, was brilliant to the point of genius. They used rallies, road signs, maps, guides and restaurant reviews and, of course, Monsieur Bibendum himself, to promote an interest in travel and hence boost the sale of their tyres. I wish Bibendum had been dreamt up by O'Conran rather than O'Gallop!

Apart from bereavements, when was the last time you cried, and what was the reason?
TIM LITTLE

I cry quite easily, especially when I'm watching films with soppy endings, but recently I found myself crying over an advertisement that Michelin had put in the *Financial Times*, celebrating the fact that Monsieur Bibendum had been recognized as the best logo in the world. All they had done was to make Bib look rather coy and blushing; it was brilliant and charming.

Contemporary advertising by Michelin, who certainly get my vote as the world's best marketeers for their work early last century. I particularly liked the fact that in the good old days Bibendum was always pictured smoking a Monte Cristo No. 2.

Bibendum voted the world's best logo.

*The Financial Times convened an international jury of 20 personalities
from the disciplines of art, communication, architecture and
design who voted Bibendum the world's best logo.
Our thanks to everyone.*

www.michelin.com

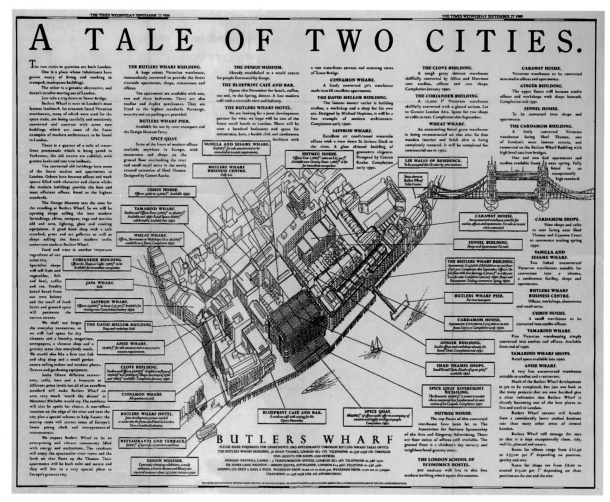

A double-page advertisement in The Times for Butlers Wharf property, which I designed.
It achieved nothing. Such was the depth of the recession.

Butlers Wharf was an outstanding opportunity. What lessons were learned?

ROGER SEELIG

The very first time I saw Butlers Wharf I knew that it was a fantastic development opportunity. Oddly enough, I initially spotted it from the river; we'd hired a riverboat for an office party and just as the boat nosed past Tower Bridge I noticed these wonderful, derelict warehouses on the south bank of the Thames. When I later managed to visit on foot, I was utterly smitten by the rough and robust Victorian industrial architecture. Many of the buildings along the waterfront and in the streets immediately behind had been used to store and grind spices and the air still smelled of them. I've always been hugely attracted by the potential of run-down, abandoned areas and I jumped at the chance to acquire the thirteen-acre site. In 1983 we formed a company with the Lords McAlpine and Rothschild as minority shareholders and managed to buy the site for £3 million, subject to planning permission.

Our architectural practice, Conran Roche, produced an excellent mixed-use scheme, which combined new buildings with sensitive restoration of the old: homes and shops, workshops and offices and a site for a design museum, a project dear to my heart. Initially, the senior architect for the scheme was Stuart Moscrop, a disciple of the Mies van der Rohe school, who was a fine designer of new minimalist buildings but fairly uninterested in the conversion of old Docklands warehouses. We had a few disagreements, mainly centred around the fact that I wanted to maximize space and minimize cost and he had rather grander ideas in mind. Fairly soon, we both realized that he was not the ideal architect for the job, so other members of the team took it over. However, he did collaborate on the design of a beautiful glass cobweb of a building with an undulating roof that we produced for Logica. The building would have been sited right on the waterfront where it would have made a wonderful complement to Tower Bridge.

On the strength of the scheme, Midland Bank lent us the money for the development, saying that it was the very best opportunity in London. In fact, in common with many over-eager financial institutions during the 1980s, they pressed us to borrow from them. We ourselves were so confident of its success that we invested heavily in new infrastructure – new roads, drainage and a new riverfront – before we had even begun to develop the warehouses. Our optimism seemed to be justified when the first apartment building that we completed sold out immediately as soon as it went on the market.

The first thing to go wrong was the extremely expensive and unpleasant discovery that the major residential building, Butlers Wharf itself, only had proper foundations at one end. Of course, the whole site had previously been surveyed, but the presence of foundations at one end must have led someone to assume that there would be foundations at the other end as well. As developers for the scheme, we had no recourse but to blame ourselves and absorb the huge cost. Adding foundations to the unsupported end naturally caused terrific delays and by the time we came to sell the apartments in the renovated Butlers Wharf building, the recession had well and truly set in. Nothing in Docklands, indeed very little in London, was saleable at any price.

As the recession deepened, Midland got cold feet about any investment relating to property. They soon called for the repayment of the loan as we could not pay the interest, then running at sixteen per cent. I suggested to the chairman that he take our shares and leave us to run the project, but he was overruled and they decided to put the development into receivership. Lord Rothschild and Lord McAlpine resigned their directorships, leaving me to face the music. I still don't know whether this was because they did not want their names to be associated with failure, or because they had simply lost interest in what was no longer going to be a success. At any rate, I missed their friendship during this very difficult time.

LEFT: *The bronze Paolozzi head being delivered to the quayside outside the Design Museum.*

BELOW: *Our proposals for Butlers Wharf included this glass cobweb of a building, which would have been Logica's headquarters. Instead, the site is now occupied by a rather lumpen apartment building.*

LEFT: *The derelict Butlers Wharf building before development. We provided, among other things, a new quay and riverside walk.*

Now, nearly twenty years after we first bought the site, the project is reaching completion. Although it doesn't match up to our original ideas for a true 'mixed-use development, it has eventually become one of the most successful of all Docklands regenerations and has helped put Southwark on the map.

What have we learned?

To pre-sell property before making a large commitment. To tie banks into long-term loans with a fix on interest rates or a roll up of interest if required. To have an excellent financial director in place and property agents who share the developer's enthusiasm for the project. To always remain aware that there could be a recession around the corner.

We both share a great affection for Butlers Wharf and some regret that the last recession prevented the construction of your original vision of a true mixed-use community. Much delay was caused by the planning authority and English Heritage, and if they'd been more helpful we might have built much more before the slump in the market. I would love to bring some of them back here now to see the results of their delays (many incompetent pastiche warehouses). What do you think of the way planners and heritage groups control our built environment?
PAUL ZARA

All of us who were involved in the original planning of Butlers Wharf cannot help but be sad that our dream of a mixed-use site, with excellent modern buildings interleaved with the sensitive restoration of old buildings, never happened. I am particularly depressed that the Southwark planners have gone on to allow so much second- or even third-rate architecture to be built. When the LDDC ran the show, they were determined that only the best would do. Certainly the delays caused by planners, English Heritage and the general planning bureaucracy, coinciding with the recession, caused companies like Logica to pull out of the project.

While Butlers Wharf is a financially successful development today, aesthetically and in terms of creating a unique community it is something of a failure. I still dream of what it could have been but I doubt if the planners share the vision or, indeed, really care.

When I first met you (in 1991) you had a fearsome reputation – rightly so, from what I saw! What has mellowed you?

SIMON WILLIS

The year 1991 was not a good time for me. I was very frustrated in several areas of my career. My involvement with Storehouse had just come to an end, Butlers Wharf was in receivership, and I was trying to make a new life for myself in quite difficult circumstances.

For a while, it seemed that things could only get worse. Fred Roche, who was in charge of our architectural practice, had died of cancer as we were struggling to keep Butlers Wharf out of receivership. By 1993, after a couple of years of recession, the practice was in a very precarious state. Stuart Moscrop, who had taken over Fred's role, went out to Jamaica to meet Chris Blackwell, founder of Island Records, who had been introduced to us by a friend of mine, and discuss a possible job to design a hotel in Miami. When he returned, he came to see me, announced he was leaving and took the job with him.

The timing was unfortunate, to say the least. On the previous day, our thirtieth wedding anniversary, Caroline had also announced that she was leaving me. It was a tremendous shock. We had never really had rows, and our relationship had evolved to the point where we both were able to do things we were interested in without, I thought, a great deal of conflict. But it had become clear that she deplored the 'big business' side of my life, a side that has not dominated my career since Storehouse.

All the while I was opening the restaurants and shops that comprise the Butlers Wharf gastrodrome and had just opened Quaglino's, a thrilling project but rather nail-biting to execute. Certainly there was plenty on my mind, which could well have made me seem rather fearsome.

But who says I've mellowed?

RESTAURANTS

Although I owned restaurants in the 1950s, these were chiefly the means to an end and the money they made was invested in my furniture-making business. For nearly twenty years, the cockroach was dormant in my bloodstream until 1971, when I moved my design business to Neal Street, Covent Garden. An empty space on the ground floor of our converted warehouse seemed the perfect place for a restaurant to entertain our clients and show off our design skills. It's been owned and run by my brother-in-law, Antonio Carluccio, since 1985.

Over the years many of our shops included cafés, but our conversion of the Michelin Building provided the opportunity to attempt something more gastronomically ambitious. The result was Bibendum, opened in 1987, and still rated as one of the best places to eat in London. Blue Print Café, on the first floor of the Design Museum, opened two years later.

With the development of Butlers Wharf, I seized the chance to create what I called a 'gastrodrome', where restaurants, wine merchants, food shops, cafés and bars created a destination; the same idea informed our development of Bluebird in the King's Road. Today, we have forty-two restaurants, cafés, bars, clubs and food markets all over the world, ranging from expensive to affordable and the grandly theatrical to the more intimate. This expansion, which many people seem to regard as amounting to my second career, to me seems a perfectly natural extension of my lifelong interests in food, design, interiors, buildings and offering people new choices and experiences.

Post-Storehouse, late in life and in the teeth of a recession, it was a brave move to embark upon your restaurant empire, but weren't you tempted to rest on your laurels?
RODNEY KINSMAN

Resting on laurels or indeed any other bush is not my idea of enjoying myself. I love new projects and I think I always will to my dying day. When I opened Le Pont de la Tour at Butlers Wharf, I think people thought I was mad rather than brave. I was constantly told that no one would ever cross the river to eat lunch, much less dinner. Even people in the restaurant business thought it was a strange thing to do. I was having lunch recently with Chris Corbin and Jeremy King and they remembered coming down to see the show flat at Butlers Wharf when the area was still quite derelict. I insisted that they take a look at the space on the ground floor of the main warehouse where I was planning to create Le Pont de la Tour. They said that going back in a taxi afterwards they were belly-laughing, saying I'd really lost it!

EGON RONAY:
What gave you the courage to open your first very big restaurant, Quaglino's, in a then-unfashionable dining-out district and expect that it would be filled by some four hundred or more customers nightly?

Opening Quaglino's at the depth of the recession was seen as pretty outrageous, certainly by other restaurateurs. I had been to most of the grand brasseries in Paris and had observed that they were almost always packed with a democratic, buzzy crowd – young and old, the well-off and less well-off – and I thought, why shouldn't this work in London? Those in the know greeted my ideas with scepticism and I was expressly told by several people that if Londoners had felt the need for a large restaurant there would already be one. London now has several, all of them doing pretty well, it seems. I think it is really a case of nothing ventured, nothing gained.

How did you solve the hard problem of providing a high level of culinary quality in your giant establishments like Quaglino's and Mezzo?

We looked at large restaurants and brasseries in France, such as La Coupole in Paris, and analysed how they produced good food on a grand scale. Then we modernized many of their ideas. Computerized ordering systems, such as Remanco, have made the communication of information so much simpler and more efficient in recent years. But the real secret is to employ excellent chefs, to use only high quality ingredients and to have good management.

LEFT: *Having a few with Charles Campbell, manager of The Neal Street Restaurant in its early days. A great bon viveur, Charles was occasionally known to greet customers with his trousers round his ankles. One of the nicest men in the world, even when pissed.*

BELOW: *The café in the Dordogne where Kasmin and I wrote the first menus for The Neal Street Restaurant over several bottles of Alsace.*

ABOVE LEFT: *Le Pont de la Tour, Butlers Wharf.*

ABOVE: *The two kitchens, one above the other, at Mezzo, Soho.*

LEFT: *The grand staircase at Quaglino's with kaleidoscopic ceiling and walls.*

Some time ago I asked you what drove you to keep opening restaurant after restaurant and when you hesitated I suggested that it wasn't money. What is it?

People in any business develop and quite often look for a greater challenge. In a restaurant, a sous chef often has the ambition to become a head chef; a head waiter to become a manager. If a business does not provide opportunities for such people to move up the ladder they will leave. Our policy has always been to try and create new challenges for our staff by opening new places. That said, the truth of the matter is that we love new projects and new ideas. It keeps everybody on their toes.

As you cannot be impervious to unjust, harping criticism in newspaper columns now and again about the quality of food in some of your establishments, what is your frank and outspoken reaction to such baseless remarks?

It really depends on the critic as to how seriously we take their remarks. Sometimes criticism is justified and we are grateful that our shortcomings have been pointed out so that we can take action to correct the situation. Sadly, however, there seem to be quite a few critics who write outrageous and inaccurate reviews to amuse their readers or to gain publicity. The restaurant guide Harden's, for example, has a crack at us every year, which always seems to guarantee them extra press coverage. It would be amusing if it didn't affect the morale of our excellent staff. Bizarrely, a bad review can often increase business in a restaurant, which may show either that the public doesn't take restaurant reviews very seriously or that there is no such thing as bad publicity! In the end, you simply have to accept that the critics' slings and arrows are just part of the business.

Restaurateurs have no vehicle for responding to the critics, or indeed for commenting on the behaviour of their customers. 'No show', for example, is a major problem that nobody wants to face up to. Customers book several restaurants and turn up to the one they most fancy for lunch or dinner, making no effort to cancel the other bookings. This happens frequently and can financially ruin a small restaurant. Then there are the professional complainers who ring up the next day and say that they have been sick all night and want a refund. When the restaurant asks for medical confirmation, everything goes quiet. Food or wine is dropped on clothes on purpose to claim cleaning bills or even replacement clothes. Extraordinary damage is done, especially to lavatories and loose furniture. Anything that is not bolted down will get stolen; even things that are screwed to the wall, like coathooks, lavatory paper dispensers and door knobs, get unscrewed. Thousands of ashtrays, huge quantities of cutlery, china, glass vases full of flowers, sculptures and paintings, napkins, tablecloths, you name it, it goes.

These are just a few of the downsides that tend not to be mentioned by the restaurant critics. The upside, of course, is that it is an enormous pleasure to see a restaurant filled with people having a great time and everything working like clockwork. Nine-tenths of our customers are wonderful and some of them even write to say they have had a good time.

JULIE RICHARDSON:
Do you complain in other people's restaurants if things aren't up to scratch?

I would never make a fuss. I would ask to see the general manager and explain calmly that something was wrong and ask politely if he or she could put it right. Running a restaurant is very difficult and things inevitably go wrong from time to time. I have always found that reasonable complaints are welcome.

If you could 'do away' with somebody, how would you do it (and who would it be)?

Keith Hobbs, slowly. Keith had worked as a junior on The Neal Street Restaurant back in the early 1970s and had come to work with me again as a freelance consultant when we were developing the Gastrodrome, Quaglino's and Mezzo. He was a good contract administrator, very lively and buoyant, and was very effective at running complicated jobs. I'd even given him some shares in Quaglino's. When we decided to merge our interior design side with the architectural practice, Keith kept finding reasons not to join us as a full-time employee. Then we discovered why. He had set up his own design group in the building next door, siphoning off some of our clients and staff, while continuing to give the impression he was working with us. We did not part on the best of terms.

How would you cook Michael Winner if you had the opportunity and who would you serve up for pudding?
MAGGIE HEANEY

Trussed, stuffed and simmered, like *gigot à sept heures*. A A Gill might make a fetchingly sweet little accompanying dish, well caramelized and crisp around the edges. Both of them fine examples from the Wapping force-feeding farm; both certain to cause indigestion. Who would eat them is quite another question. I suspect they would both get consigned to the deep freeze and forgotten.

With your immense creative instincts, what inspires you the most when you are about to introduce a new concept?

ROSE MARIE BRAVO

When I see happy customers enjoying what we've done it inspires me to move on to the next project. Soon after Quaglino's opened, I remember standing on the balcony and looking down over the packed dining room, with waiters carrying huge trays balanced over their heads, darting around between the tables. A happy buzz wafted around the huge space. In my exhausted state I thought, 'this is wonderful'. It was a battle won, so on to the next.

Why are your restaurants so noisy?

MICHAEL GRADE

Out of our forty-two restaurants, cafés, bars and clubs, four are noisy. The noisy ones are Quaglino's, Bluebird, Mezzo and downstairs at Guastavino's. They're noisy partly because they are large and partly because they are not particularly soft or upholstered places; the point is to re-create the atmosphere of the huge Parisian brasseries, large, bustling, energetic places that have been part of Parisian life for the last hundred years. It's true that they aren't places to go if you want a quiet, intimate lunch or dinner but many people relish the buzz, particularly if they're in the mood to celebrate.

Why did the Bluebird Club not catch people's imaginations?

RUPERT HAMBRO

When we started Bluebird Club, we made it too elitist and asked for too much money as an annual subscription. Consequently, we had too few members. No one likes being in a half-empty club; people want to be in a place that is busy and successful. We lowered the entrance fee and widened the membership, simplified a lot of things so they were less pretentious and we now have a success on our hands.

What makes restaurants like Bibendum, The Neal Street Restaurant, The Ivy, Chez Gérard and Pizza Express stay successful for fifteen years and more?

LAURENCE ISAACSON

Like all businesses, a restaurant has to have a philosophy that can be shared by everyone who is involved with it. The person who runs the restaurant (or group of restaurants) should be the one who either invented the philosophy in the first place or is so imbued with it that they can communicate both their dedication and passion further on down the line; their involvement must be visible to both staff and customers. Restaurants that are run without dedication and passion – or where those qualities are not properly communicated – will gradually fail.

CHRISTOPHER BODKER:
What would you say are the principal frustrations of the restaurant business?

What frustrates me most is dealing with the endless bureaucratic issues and all the rules and regulations surrounding planning, construction, food hygiene and licensing. There seem to be whole teams of people telling you what you can and can't do, as if you had

The Butlers Wharf Chop House – very British and very woody in a modern way.

a mission to poison your customers. Worse still, many of these regulations seem to conflict and if you satisfy one, you often find yourself in breach of another. When you care passionately about what you are doing, it can be quite demotivating to be treated as if you were a potential criminal. Well, I've got that off my chest!

Bearing in mind how important good people are to the restaurant business, how do you find, recruit and keep good people?

Good people, as we all know, are fundamental to the success of every business. In a service industry like the restaurant trade, however, staff really do come into close contact and dialogue with the customers.

We constantly recruit from all over the world, we keep our ears firmly pressed to the restaurant grapevine and we advertise when we have staff shortages that we can't fill internally. Because we have a number of restaurants, cafés, bars and clubs, both in the UK and abroad, we are able to offer staff a career path so there is always the opportunity for advancement.

We pay our staff well, train them well and offer bonuses and a share of the tronc, which they administer themselves. We also offer certain senior people a bonus and a share in their own restaurant. We keep everybody in the business very well informed about our financial performance, our successes and our failures. As anybody in the business knows, there has always been an enormous mobility of staff: they move from restaurant to restaurant, and from country to country to gain experience and decorate their CVs. Eventually, they settle and I'm glad to say quite a few excellent staff have decided to settle with us.

Do you subscribe to the theory that there is a limit on the restaurants that any one particular restaurateur can own?

I believe we have discovered a formula that does not cap the number of restaurants we own. Each restaurant is a separate company, with its own management, although we have a small central organization of about twenty-five people that provides a monitoring function, helps with personnel and payroll and undertakes a certain amount of central buying of basics and wines and spirits. This central organization allows us to know on a daily basis how each restaurant is performing and also monitors margins, thus removing some of the drudgery from the managers and chefs who therefore can devote more time to improving food, customer care and service. The restaurants certainly compete among themselves as well as their competitors as if they were totally independent businesses. In addition to the main restaurant group, we also have the Zinc Bar and Grill project, which will develop slowly as a group rather than as individual entities, in a similar way to Pizza Express.

If you could open a restaurant in any building in London, which would you choose?

KEN LIVINGSTONE

I think the first floor of your new Foster building, with its views over the river and the Tower of London, would be a pretty ideal setting – we could see it as an extension of our Butlers Wharf gastrodrome and you could view it as your staff canteen. What I really like, however, is finding sites in undeveloped areas, so I would love to have a crack at the amazing control room of the derelict Battersea Power Station. I've always thought the Mall was rather underused and maybe some of those spaces on the north side, which appear to be used as garages, could make very nice indoor–outdoor cafés and restaurants. The Queen and her mother could nip out for a cappuccino and a gin and tonic.

The Blairs invited the Clintons to have a family dinner at Le Pont de la Tour. Keep everything absolutely normal, said the Prime Minister. It was – except for the presence of about a thousand security guards and five hundred paparazzi.

You've equally mastered the art of business and the art of hosting lunch. But I wonder if you actually personally enjoy business lunches?

RICHARD McINTYRE

If you are at a stage in your negotiations when you appear to have reached a stalemate, then I think a good lunch or dinner can help to break a log jam. This is because a meal becomes a gesture of friendship and you talk about things other than pure business, perhaps returning at the end of the meal to try and find ways of resolving the sticking point. I certainly find that this has often helped. Eating together is also a very nice way of thanking someone who has been helpful, or indeed celebrating a successful deal. Lunch is definitely not for wimps. It's a serious way of releasing tensions and an enjoyable and efficient way of doing business.

Perhaps the ultimate example of this aspect of eating out was when the Blairs and Clintons came to Le Pont de la Tour. We had had a phone call from Downing Street saying that Tony Blair thought he would like to take President Clinton and his wife out for dinner and wondered if there was a table available at the restaurant (along with another for the security staff). We were told that the Prime Minister wished it to be an absolutely normal, relaxed occasion and that none of the people who had already booked that evening should be turned away.

The evening came and a massive security presence became evident, complete with marksmen on the rooftops. Although the British police seemed to manage it all rather elegantly, on the American side it was quite heavy-handed. (The President's security staff wouldn't let him use the normal Pont lavatories so he had to have a pee in the staff loo.) The Blairs and Clintons had a drink on the terrace outside first and then sat down to eat at a table at the end of the restaurant, with the public all around them. They evidently enjoyed themselves very much, as they overshot by an hour.

When they stood up to leave, everyone in the restaurant clapped. Then they made their way to the kitchen, where they thanked the staff and even shook hands with the washers-up. The only glitch in the evening came when the huge Clinton calvacade got onto the approach to Tower Bridge, only to find traffic at a standstill because the bridge was raised. The US security people were going crazy but the bridgemaster was adamant: he wasn't going to lower the bridge for anyone, not even the President; the Thames barge *Gladys* was booked to go through.

I stayed out of the way that evening. Joel Kissin, then managing director of the restaurant group, handled everything beautifully. I think it was one of the best moments of his life, judging from the pictures and letters he has on the wall of his office.

Excluding your own, which is your favourite restaurant interior, past or present, and do you consider the current designer/restaurant boom you virtually started is in danger of reaching saturation point?

RODNEY KINSMAN

I've always thought the Lucas Carton in Paris, along with Le Grand Vefour, the two best traditional interiors. The Four Seasons in the Seagram Building in New York is an excellent modern interior and has stood the test of time very well.

I think London is now fairly well supplied with large restaurants, but it is difficult to say whether or not we are at saturation point. Years ago, people ate out only on big occasions – to celebrate a birthday, promotion or anniversary. Today, many more people regularly eat out than ever before; it's become an accepted form of entertainment, an alternative to eating in and watching telly. Then you have to consider the high failure rate of many new enterprises: a huge proportion of restaurants fail in their first year, for a variety of reasons including simple bad luck, but mainly through lack of experience.

When you embark on a new project, what do you consider the most important criterion to make it successful?

GRACE LEO-ANDRIEU

We believe that if we can offer something different and execute it with confidence and determination, success is more likely to follow. For example, quite a lot of our new projects, particularly restaurants and shops, have been located in redundant properties, slightly off the beaten track. They may be sites that other people have rejected or those that are difficult to develop. That degree of challenge makes us all the more determined to succeed. Such sites often have low rents or cheap freeholds, and offer the potential to kickstart the regeneration of an area.

I've always been inspired by quirky, eccentric spaces and have spent a lot of my life revitalizing abandoned and derelict buildings, both for my own use and as premises for factories, shops and restaurants. Some of the early Habitats were in beautiful disused buildings – an old church in Tunbridge Wells, a 1920s cinema on the King's Road, an old Spitfire factory in Chester. Bluebird Garage was one building that I had coveted for years, ever since I opened a restaurant opposite it in 1955; it was a particular pleasure to convert it into a version of the Butlers Wharf gastrodrome, with an open-air food market, shop, restaurant, bar and club on the same site. And one of the most exciting projects in this respect was our development of Guastavino's in one of the most ravishing spaces in Manhattan under the 59th Street Bridge.

Saving an old building and giving it a new lease of life gives everybody involved a degree of pleasure that an entirely new project does not always inspire. Very often the contrast between modern design and existing architecture can be synergistic.

Is it all gut instinct or do you rely on market research to determine where, how and when to open a new shop or restaurant?
WERNER BULLEN

You need all the information you can get before you start a new project, which may well include social trends and forecasts and pieces of market research. But once you are fully informed, you need to let your gut instincts take over. In this way, the result will not simply reflect historical information, which is all that research can be. Admittedly, gut feeling is only a complex assimilation of all that you have experienced and learned in your life, but something about the process tends to lead to greater originality.

NICHOLAS RETTIE:
What inspired you to create the variety of restaurants at the Great Eastern Hotel?

Rather in the way we created the Gastrodrome at Butlers Wharf, we wanted to find a way of making a new sort of hotel, a place where there would be a variety of different entertaining activities on offer, as well as a place simply to lay one's head and sleep. With the hotel's location right next to Liverpool Street Station in the heart of the City, it was obvious

TOP: *The riverfront at the restored and revived Butlers Wharf, with its restaurants.*
ABOVE: *The Bluebird gastrodrome, created from a disused garage.*

ABOVE: *There are five restaurants at the Great Eastern Hotel, each with very different identities.*
LEFT: *The mini Guggenheim spy hole that pierces the six floors of the Great Eastern Hotel.*

that many people who came to the Great Eastern would need to work or extend their working day. This meant that rooms needed to be technically well-equipped and that a large amount of meeting rooms would have to be provided. Many people would also want to combine work and social life, which directed the way we looked at the restaurants and bars.

People today often work in a rather solitary way; the computer screen certainly dominates life in the City. We felt it was important to have a variety of different restaurants, cafés, bars, pubs and bistros, not only to create a diversity of price and atmosphere, but to give the hotel the sociable feel of a small village. In the past, to reach many hotel restaurants one would have had to pass through the hotel's main entrance, which could be an intimidating experience for those who were not hotel guests. At the Great Eastern, each restaurant or bar can be accessed either from the street or from the hotel, which helps to reinforce their different identities and draws in casual customers for a meal or a drink. I think we have succeeded in creating this sense of place.

Being a hotelier or restaurateur is certainly not for the person who wants an easy life. But the Great Eastern was an exciting project particularly because we had to find contemporary solutions to traditional activities. And, like a restaurant, every day is a new performance. The Great Eastern was a major renovation project. Now I would like to move on and create an entirely new hotel, from below the ground up to the sky.

What stimulates you about people in the hospitality business?

Oh, I hate the term 'hospitality business', just as much as 'food and beverage' and 'banqueting'. It's all so genteel. I find good staff stimulating because they really do enjoy making people happy and giving them a good time. They get pleasure and pride from being part of an efficient and cheerful team and when it all works well you can sense a contented buzz in the atmosphere. Unfortunately, the hotel and restaurant business also attracts its fair share of misfits who do their best to disrupt the professionalism of the team. Pass them on to your competitors as quickly as possible; even better, persuade them to look for another career path.

Do you consider yourself more successful as a restaurateur than a shopkeeper and if so, why?

JOHN SAINSBURY

I have always thought that there are great similarities between the retailing and restaurant businesses. The food production side in restaurants draws on the expertise of both manufacture, supply lines and warehousing with all the controls, especially of quality, also necessary in retailing. Front of house is about creating an ambience and customer care, plus of course the presentation and pricing of the product. Having spent time with you going around the shelves of Savacentre, I know that your attention to detail, awareness of customers and staff and, in particular, your interest in the quality and the appearance of food and its presentation, would make you a pretty good restaurateur, just in case you are looking for a new career opportunity! I think I am reasonably good at both businesses but I see no major dividing line between either activity.

It seems that you have always had a burning passion for the world of food and, like a true Amphitryon, you are fascinated by the inexhaustible play of culinary sensations and emotions. However, all this could have remained your secret garden of art and curiosities. What enticed you to translate this passion into a dynamic business? What secret induced you to transform it into an industrial concept perfectly focused and which, somehow, reminds one of certain successes of *haute couture*?

MICHEL GUÉRARD

Rather like you, I enjoy the pleasure of entertaining people and offering them a slice of my life. But I think you offer rather more of the *haute couture* experience than we do. Our restaurants are more of a diffusion or *prêt-à-porter* business. I suppose one might call your Ferme aux Grives a Guérard diffusion; I wish there were more of them around France. Here in Britain we would certainly receive them with open arms.

I have always seen our restaurants and, more recently, our hotel, as a natural progression from our home furnishings stores, in much the same way, I imagine, as you see your hotels, vineyard and spa following on from your restaurants. I've always thought of you and your books as France's answer to Elizabeth David.

What time of your life did you find the most stimulating, creatively? (Apart from the time with me!)

GEORGE DAVIES

From the mid-1990s onwards was a very stimulating and creative time; there was a great buzz in the office. We had a large number of new restaurant projects on the go; The Conran Shop was expanding in France and Japan; we were doing our first studies on the Bridgemarket project in New York and the Great Eastern Hotel in London; and we were also working on the design of products that would form the basis of the Conran Collection range. Today, one of the things that really keeps the creative juices flowing is Benchmark, our furniture business based at Barton Court. I can design something on Monday and have a working prototype by Friday.

When did you have the most fun in your career and why?

MICHAEL BLOOMBERG

The end of 1998 and most of 1999 was exhausting, terrifying and great fun. This period marked the culmination of many projects around the world that we had been working on for some time: the Great Eastern Hotel in London, Bern's in Stockholm; Alcazar, my first restaurant in Paris; the Bridgemarket development comprising Guastavino's and The Conran Shop in Manhattan. Life was a whirlwind: battles with builders; staff interviews, employment and training; plotting PR and advertising campaigns; stocking shops; restaurant testing and more testing. I was constantly jumping on and off planes, and never knew where I was going to wake up next. Then, when everything was finally ready, there were the opening parties and press interviews. All in all, it was heaven and hell at the same time, but chiefly heaven, because there is nothing more exciting than seeing something you have planned and worked on for many years finally come together and start trading. Both the Great Eastern and the Bridgemarket developments had been in the works for four years, so you can imagine the sighs of relief.

Many other things also fell into place around the same time. I established my office at Barton Court, which allows me the time and space to be more of a designer and less of an agony aunt. And, for the last time, I also got married, to Vicki, with whom I have been happier than ever.

I had met Vicki about six years earlier in the south of France. I was in Nice to give a lecture at an enormous conference on retailing in the food industry, but on the day of the lecture Air France went on strike and I had had the slightly demotivating experience of speaking to a half-empty hall. It was about six months after the split with Caroline and I was fairly low and depressed generally. In the evening I was sitting in the bar of the hotel where

I was staying, feeling rather gloomy and wondering if I could even be bothered to go out to dinner, when an Englishman I had met at the conference came in and asked me to join him for a drink. He asked me to keep an eye out for a blonde he'd arranged to have dinner with. 'There's your blonde,' I told him, when a woman came into the bar. But it wasn't the right one. Eventually the right 'blonde' arrived, quite late. It was Vicki.

We all ended up having dinner together; I remember we had a very good plate of *osso bucco* – but I also remember that Vicki and I flirted outrageously. She was living in Nice at that time with her three children and employed by Bono to supervise a large design scheme on site. She'd separated from her husband and come to France to get a better education for her children. After dinner we went on to the Iguana, a Cuban club in the harbour where someone had been knifed on the doorstep a couple of nights before, had an incredibly jolly time and got on together very well. The next weekend I flew out to Nice to see her and within two months we'd decided to live together.

You often remark that quite a lot of food served in restaurants, particularly those of the Michelin star persuasion, is too complicated and over-garnished, and that frequently the dishes have a superfluity of ingredients. At home, we eat simply, albeit sometimes quite luxuriously, using very good ingredients and lots of fresh vegetables from the garden. If you were going to start again in the restaurant business, what sort of dishes would you like to have on the menu?
VICKI CONRAN

As you know, I'm constantly railing against restaurant food that is overcomplicated, ditzed around with, and buried and surrounded by irrelevant garnishes. For some reason, chefs with stars in their eyes believe that they have to decorate food to add value for their

customers and impress the restaurant guides. They feel emasculated if they present good quality ingredients that are simply cooked and simply served. They dream of making their names by inventing dishes that mix this with that and just a pinch of the other. If they can also go on to present the dish so that it looks like the Leaning Tower of Pisa or a piazza in Siena, they have confirmed to themselves that they are really more of a conceptual artist than a cook and that TV appearances and bestselling cookbooks must be just around the corner. The result is confusion on a plate, where nothing tastes of anything. If only such chefs spent the money they waste on labour in the kitchen on better quality ingredients instead, I'd be a happier man.

For my ideal restaurant, I'd look for good cooks rather than chefs, I'd source the best possible ingredients, serve generous portions on plain oval, heavy porcelain serving dishes so that customers could help themselves, and my only garnish would be a bunch of shiny, large-leafed watercress with some of the meat and birds. All ingredients would be in season as far as possible. My menu would be drawn from a list of classic French standards and the best British produce and I would not offer much more than twenty dishes at any one time.

Do you think that we have become neurotic about food safety?

JEREMY LEE

I am constantly amazed at the advice given by the Food Safety Agency. They seem to spend their lives trying to destroy all known bacteria without recognizing that some of these self-same bacteria are essential in fighting the battle for us if we do eat food that disagrees with us. Such is their desire to pump us full of antibiotics and see that our food is clinically clean that we risk becoming seriously ill if, for instance, we eat couscous in a kasbah on our package holiday to Tangier. The old saying that 'you have to eat a peck of dirt before you die' has some wisdom in it.

Obviously, our restaurants have to comply fully with FSA edicts, and maintain high standards of hygiene that are strictly observed and monitored. But despite all the rules and regulations, there are still plenty of restaurants and cafés where food is prepared in squalid conditions. Considering we're a nation well on the way to having our immune systems completely sterilized, it's surprising we are not dying like flies.

It's pretty obvious that I do not have a scientific approach to food safety, just a lifetime of eating and drinking anything and everything, without regard for hyper-hygiene. I seek out unpasteurized milk, cream and butter because it tastes better. I am not the slightest bit concerned about a caterpillar in my salad (they eat grubs in Thailand) and have often enjoyed food that is well past its sell-by date (it usually tastes better).

Terence, you like red wine. Could you imagine selling Austrian or Hungarian wines in your restaurants?

ZOLTAN OSZKO

To answer your question, I have had some really excellent Austrian wine; I've also had some awful wines in Austria. Recently I went to a tasting at the Trieste Hotel in Vienna and we now have about twenty different Austrian wines on the lists of our various restaurants. My favourite is Pinot Noir Pittnauer Alte Reben. I'm afraid our only Hungarian wine is the delicious Tokaji Puttonyos.

In recent years, I have also enjoyed wine from many other countries, particularly Spain, Italy and Australia, as the quality has improved so dramatically. Rather boringly I usually drink red wine with meat or game, and white with fish, shellfish or vegetables. I like Alsace wines with sauerkraut and shellfish and champagne before the meal, rather than with it.

I do like wine and tend to drink it with every meal, except breakfast (but I don't always eat much then, which is probably the reason for its exclusion). My favourite wines are still Burgundies, both white and red, and marc de Bourgogne. Like most people, I like to drink local wine (and eat regional food) when I am in a wine-producing area or country. Taking into account food, wine and architecture, Burgundy remains my favourite region in France, especially the beautiful countryside and small villages along the canal. The old semi-industrial buildings associated with wine production are just as magnificent as the châteaux.

Speaking of old red wines, I was once having dinner with some friends and we were discussing how wine from a good maker was always decent, even if the year was not particularly good. I looked at the wine list and spotted a magnum of Château Latour 1955 for FF500, while the 1956 was FF5,000. It seemed the perfect opportunity to put our theory to the test. When the bottle was brought to the table, the sommelier carefully decanted the wine and apologized for the fact that it had lost its label. We tasted it and all agreed it was truly marvellous for 1955. Later, the proprietor of the restaurant came by to ask us how we were enjoying the wine. Then he showed us the cork, which read 1956. When we went back the next day and had the 1955 magnum, we had to admit that, although it was good, there was really no comparison.

Which wine do you serve with asparagus?

BILL BAKER

I was once a guest at a dinner given by a wine merchant. We had magnums of 1945 Château Margaux, Château Latour, Château Lafite-Rothschild and Château Pétrus. His wife served asparagus, followed by artichoke soufflé. I believe they got divorced soon after. So if I did drink anything with asparagus, it would be cheap, white and dry; I have also had Gewürztraminer, which worked quite well.

My ideal way of shopping is to browse through open-air markets, such as those in France, Italy or Spain. The essential precursor of a good meal.

Name the time and place of your best Martini cocktail ever.

JAMES SOANE

I can't name a time, but the King Cole bar with its wonderful mural in the otherwise awful St Regis Hotel in New York makes star quality Martinis with Tanqueray gin. The Martinis at Quaglino's are also ace – the secret is to keep all the ingredients, and the glass, in the freezer. Try Plymouth gin as the base: it's the best.

The Japanese haven't changed their style, nor the Chinese, nor the Spanish. Do you think the French should change their style and move towards fusion food?

RAYMOND BLANC

We're all increasingly influenced by what we see and taste from all over the world. Fifteen years ago we had an exhibition at the Boilerhouse called 'National Characteristics', and those significant differences that we then detected between countries would be harder to spot now.

The style of eating is gradually changing in Japan and Spain, but rather than tamper with their traditional dishes, they seem to be offering a greater variety of different types of food. If you go to Hong Kong or Shanghai, you can see that the Chinese view the world as their oyster: anything and everything is available.

I think that it is very important that the French should not forget their simple, traditional food; the quality of French produce, from the countryside or the sea, is the best in the world. Recently, I believe that *nouvelle cuisine* and fast food have really damaged and confused French taste buds. And the thirty-five-hour week, which makes it difficult for restaurants to be run in their traditional way, hasn't helped either. Some of that essential generosity that made French restaurants such a pleasure to visit seems to have been lost. However, French chefs should be just as prepared to move forward as their American, Australian and British counterparts, as you have demonstrated so successfully.

What is your favourite restaurant in France?

BILL BAKER

In terms of food and service, Paul Bocuse in Lyon is sublime. I wish I could go on to mention all those simple bistros and brasseries where for many years I have had perfect, classic French cooking, served in an unpretentious way, on plain, heavy white plates, but these are fast disappearing as the 'MacDo' mentality sweeps through France and nothing much that I enjoy seems to be replacing them. L'Ami Louis is still good for a blowout, as I'm sure you'd agree.

The terrace at l'Oustau de Baumanière at Les Baux in Provence. Perfect apart from the chairs.

You've won the dream weekend in France. Please nominate the hotel and (very important) the choice of car to take you there. Also, describe the menu for dinner on Saturday night with Vicki.

PETER BLOND

Maybe it's old age, but I would take Vicki to a place I know quite well called l'Oustau de Baumanière at Les Baux, in Provence. It's a hotel in the Val d'Enfer, which has lots of little self-contained houses in the grounds providing additional accommodation; there is a beautiful indoor–outdoor restaurant in the main hotel and the food is pretty good, too. We would stay in one of the little houses that have recently been sensitively refurbished and walk up to the restaurant with the amazing sculptured rocks of Les Petits Alpilles towering over our heads.

We would eat on the terrace with the huge blue pool in front of us. Champagne cocktail to start, then a pigeon terrine with celeriac and *foie gras en gelée*. The classic Baumanière dish, invented by Jean-André Charial's grandfather, Raymond Thuillier, is a small gigot of milk-fed local lamb *en croute* served with some of the tiniest vegetables you have ever seen, which they grow themselves. Very small but full of flavour. The cheese trolley is amazing; we would probably have a runny Saint Marcellin, then perhaps some *fraises du bois*.

One of the star attractions of the Baumanière is its huge wine list, built up over the last fifty years or so, which features lots of old red Burgundy at quite reasonable prices. So we'd have one of those and a bottle of something younger and fresher and white to begin with. Then coffee for me and a marc de Bourgogne plus an excellent cigar from Serge's hoard; a glass of champagne for Vicki.

I'd drive my Porsche 911 soft top, unless you offered to chauffeur us in an old Lancia, Lagonda or Bentley, or anything else romantic you'd got on the stocks at Sotheby's – in which case you could also come to dinner!

One might say that you are just as well known a bon viveur as Monsieur Bibendum. Has there ever been a time in your life when you have been made to fast? Was it or would it be a difficult thing to do? Do you think there should be a time set aside for all of us when we should abstain from some form of eating or drinking?
GRAHAM WILLIAMS

I'm writing the reply to your question on New Year's Eve, exactly the right moment to contemplate the year ahead. I have to say I hope next year does not include any Lenten fasting for me. However, I do think it is a good idea to be able to control your intake and to have enough strength of character to give up certain things if they are obviously not agreeing with you. I have seen many people go on dramatic diets, lose huge amounts of weight and then put it all on again in a matter of weeks after celebrating the success of their regime.

I have been overweight by the same amount for the last forty years and I expect I will remain so. Even if my doctor told me to, I doubt I would ever fast. Happiness, peace of mind and a full stomach make you look forward to tomorrow. As they say, at the age of seventy a penny saved is a penny wasted. You could say the same of a lamb chop and a glass of Burgundy.

There are no homes in the country and London, no extraordinary empire of design practices, international retail shops, restaurants or employees. Therefore none of the things you have spent a lifetime creating.

However, looking on the bright side, you do have £1,000 to your name. Now, what would you do?
SAM NEWMAN

When I was twenty-one, I started out with £300, which is rather more than £1,000 in today's money. However, I now have lots of experience, which I certainly didn't then. Provided my reputation has remained reasonably intact, I suppose I might be able to supplement that £1,000 with a loan or credit from suppliers, both of which are much easier to obtain today than back in the 1950s. If I haven't got a reputation to go on, I think things would be pretty difficult!

I think I would try and persuade somebody to rent me a failed country pub, near a reasonably affluent area, with a period of at least six months rent-free. Assuming there was a basic working kitchen, I'd tart the place up with coloured paint, strip out all the rubbish, grow vegetables in the patch at the back or front, arrange credit with butchers, bakers, fishmongers and wine merchants, and offer a simple menu with generous portions. Takings from the punters, I hope, would help to keep debtors from the door and provide the cash flow that keeps every restaurant business afloat.

Vicki and I would take turns working in the kitchen and front of house. I'd phone all the local media and send them menus and tell them the story of my downfall and modest return. People would then come to eat and gawp! Whether I could achieve this on £1,000 is very doubtful, but I would try and supplement my income by writing restaurant columns and other acerbic commentaries on contemporary life.

I am flattered to be asked to ask a question. However, I shall pass up the opportunity to do so, and simply turn to my edition of the works of Shelley and reread 'Ozymandias'.

MATTHEW FORT

I met a traveller from an antique land
Who said: Two vast and trunkless legs of stone
Stand in the desert ... Near them, on the sand,
Half sunk, a shattered visage lies, whose frown,
And wrinkled lip, and sneer of cold command,
Tell that its sculptor well those passions read
Which yet survive, stamped on these lifeless things,
The hand that mocked them, and the heart that fed:
And on the pedestal these words appear:
'My name is Ozymandias, king of kings:
Look on my works, ye Mighty, and despair!'
Nothing beside remains. Round the decay
Of that colossal wreck, boundless and bare
The lone and level sands stretch far away.

You are right to identify me as a symbol of human vanity and futility. However, it seems better to try and do something with one's life in this world. If you don't, what's the point of being here?

DESIGN

Despite the fact that I am now better known for my restaurants than anything else, I still consider myself a designer first and foremost. Design, for me, is the point at which all my other activities cross-fertilize; I've done very little in my career that neatly falls into a separate compartment.

My first design group, which I started in 1956, was a way of tying different aspects of my furniture and textile enterprises together. From the outset, this group also worked independently for outside clients and grew to be one of the most successful and profitable sides of the business.

When I had to leave the Conran Design Group behind after demerging from Ryman's, I started another group, Conran Associates, who similarly worked for outside clients as well as coming up with new shop interiors and products for Habitat; when Habitat began its major programme of expansion I set up a separate, smaller team at Barton Court in 1976 to concentrate solely on product development. After 1981, the Habitat–Mothercare Group design focused on shop and product design, while Conran Associates handled work for outside clients. I also set up Conran Roche, an architectural practice, with Fred Roche, who had been the chief executive of the Milton Keynes Development Corporation.

Today, Conran & Partners works in all spheres of design: architecture, interiors, products and graphics. Creative director of the products and graphics team is my son Sebastian, who merged his own design group with us in 1999. Over the years our design activities have been incredibly varied, from the interior of the Land Rover 'Discovery' to plastic products for Crayonne. One of my first jobs was designing offices for Michael Heseltine's Haymarket Publishing; today, nearly half a century later, we are again involved in a range of office projects for Haymarket.

Part of our design office at Hanway Place, London, circa 1966.

Other recent projects include the masterplanning of Edinburgh's waterfront and development of Ocean Terminal, a huge retail and leisure complex; the redesign of the Concorde Room at JFK and Heathrow Airports and a housing project in central Tokyo. One of our most high-profile jobs, however, came in 1997 when we were asked to fit out a space in Canary Wharf for the Anglo-French summit; we had just fifteen days, from appointment to completion. In the case of our own restaurants, shops or products, where the client is effectively ourselves, we are able to exert a high degree of control over every aspect of the project in question, a luxury many designers can't afford.

Posters for our furniture and fabrics companies in the early 1960s.

What ten qualities must a designer have to succeed? And one useful vice?

MARY QUANT

Intelligence, imagination, creativity, common sense, perseverance, market awareness, determination, skill, sensitivity *and* a thick skin, self-confidence.

I'm afraid that some of the above appear to cancel each other out, but it seems to me that they are all necessary attributes at different times and in different situations.

I suppose envy can be a useful vice, as it can act as a spur to do better and achieve more. I regret that I have been envious from time to time, particularly at the beginning of my career. In fact, I was rather envious of you and Alexander because your work was so well recognized from the start, while I was still welding away in a back room somewhere; you always appeared to spin glamorously through life not worrying about bills the way the rest of us seemed to do. And I was also pretty jealous of the fact that Robin Day had the manufacturer Hille behind him at an early stage in his career and was able to produce work in a much more sophisticated way.

What is it about the way your mind works that makes you so different and successful?

SEBASTIAN CONRAN

I don't think my mind works any differently to other designers, but I've always been very concerned with what one might call the practical aspects of design and have tried to relate most of my work to the manufacturing process.

Which of your multifaceted activities offer you the most satisfaction?

JOHN RITBLAT

My greatest satisfaction is being able to combine design, manufacture and retailing so that the products get presented to the customer in a controlled way, from the factory gate to the customer's front door. It's the same with restaurants: we find and develop the site, design the interior, decide on the type of food we want to serve and hire and train the staff. It's the holistic nature of this approach that gives me the greatest degree of satisfaction.

All my various activities — food, furniture, interior design, architecture and gardening — merge into an attitude to a style of life. I try to explain my ideas in the books I write and, to some extent, through the work of the Design Museum. I believe that intelligent design can improve the quality of life, if that doesn't sound too pious. After all, I think it is what the Design Council has been trying to achieve since the war with varying degrees of success.

Bauhaus design and architecture had a huge influence on me. Masters' houses at the Dessau Bauhaus, designed by Walter Gropius (ABOVE); Bauhaus high spirits (LEFT).

What are the connections between design and business?

EAMES DEMETRIOS

I've always thought that design was ninety-eight per cent common sense and two per cent aesthetics. It's the same for business, except that the magic ingredient is vision. Design and business are totally interlinked; and one cannot succeed without the other.

Do you think design in this country has been badly served industrially and is that the fault of the moneymen or is it the fault of engineers and marketeers? Can you identify why graphic and media design in Britain has been so commercially successful, when our product designers almost to a man/woman have had to go to continental, American and Japanese manufacturers?

CHARLES KEEN

I think that one of the answers to your questions goes back to the Industrial Revolution and the stigma attached to 'trade'. As we all know, Britain was once the workshop of the world; the synergy of engineering, design, architecture and manufacturing produced many remarkable solutions that were stunningly inventive: think of Brunel's bridges, or Paxton's Crystal Palace. But the persistent snobbery that greeted anyone with a commercial connection acted as a powerful disincentive and, I believe, prevented many people from making their careers in this sector of the economy rather than, say, the professions, the church or the army. In countries like the United States, on the other hand, success in industry was a route to the top.

In more recent times, an unfortunate twist was given to this deep-seated prejudice by successive Tory governments under Margaret Thatcher, who appeared to believe that Britain could rely on service industries alone, and by the City's financial short-termism. This clear signal from the powers-that-be that they had no faith in the future of manufacturing further depressed an already seriously damaged sector. Manufacturers knew that the best way to compete with Far Eastern companies and their reliance on cheap labour was to equip their factories with the latest automated and computerized machinery, but raising investment when the government and most banks saw no future for manufacturing was difficult to say the least. The best people left industry and the decline escalated.

In such circumstances, it is difficult for design to flourish. Design relies on a partnership with manufacturing and when manufacturers lack the confidence to invest, there is very little opportunity for designers to innovate. Graphic and media designers have been immune to this dismal trend largely because they are a service industry and because any career attached to the media has its own cachet.

The picture is not entirely gloomy. A number of foreign companies have set up very well equipped manufacturing plants in this country, demonstrating that things can still be made in Britain. There are also a number of new initiatives, such as the often-cited Dyson, where designers, engineers and manufacturers have demonstrated their entrepreneurialism to great effect.

Some brilliant young British designers now work in French *haute couture*. How do you conceive the future Europe through the prism of culture? And do you know the new generation of French designers called *les enfants de Starck*?

JACK LANG

I think France's acceptance and encouragement of young British designers into its holy of holies demonstrates how Europe can develop as a union. Cross-cultural activity is one of the best ways to bring people together and elevates the opportunities for everybody in the community, whatever activity they wish to pursue. Let's hope it won't be too long before everyone gets paid in the same currency, too.

Recently we had an exhibition at our new Conran Shop in New York that featured the work of a number of young French designers – Christian Biecher, Ronan and Erwan Bouroullec, Jean-Marie Massaud and Christophe Pillet. Along with Matali Crasset and Jérôme Olivet, these *enfants de Starck* are producing some exciting and innovative work. I think that it's excellent Philippe has created such a following. Success has a habit of breeding success and Starck's outstanding achievements worldwide have made him one of France's most important ambassadors. You should make him your next President!

You have defined more than anyone the look and style of the home in the UK in the late twentieth century. You raised our sights. Was this your ambition? You may recall, as I do with pleasure, your excitement at seeing furniture that you had personally designed in my office at the BBC.

JOHN BIRT

The most rewarding thing for designers is to see their products in use. Even today, I still get a tingle of pleasure. My original ambition was to make intelligently designed products available to anybody who might like them, without price being a barrier. As a lifelong socialist of the Burgundy variety, I have always believed that design has a part to play in democratizing a nation's taste. This all sounds a bit pretentious – perhaps the simple truth is that I enjoy designing and selling things that I like.

This range of porcelain, made in Bangladesh at a very good price, is one of my favourite products out of all those we have created. Plain, simple, useful and good for restaurants, too.

How much has your work been influenced by your personal choice, your taste, and how much by your search for something that is beautiful and functional, irrespective of personal preference?
ARABELLA LENNOX-BOYD

The majority of my design work by far has been a reflection of my own personal choice and taste. This is certainly the case when I'm designing for our own shops and restaurants or our building developments or our furniture factory, Benchmark. When it comes to work for outside clients, through Conran & Partners, the client's brief is an important consideration.

In most cases, the client is employing us to design a project for them because they like our style and reputation, and therefore we can usually design things that still retain our own personality. In some instances, we also help to write the brief. No designer enjoys compromise, but with experience one learns how to adapt one's ideal solution into something that meets the brief. If the budget takes the icing off the gingerbread, it can still taste good.

For me, you have the perfect eye in the way some people have a perfect ear. Where does this come from? Can you be trained to get it? Are there rules?
GHISLAINE BAVOILLOT

I think to some extent 'having an eye' comes with the genes. But it can also be developed like other forms of intelligence and sensitivity by education, practice and passion. If children are encouraged to be interested in visual matters, it is amazing how often such latent skills can be prodded into action.

Being receptive to the influences of other people is part of what having an 'eye' is all about. In my case, it happens all the time and I can't really identify one single most rewarding example, unless you count 'France', which I learned to love through the incomparable eye of Michael Wickham, or 'Italy', which I discovered through the eyes of Eduardo Paolozzi.

What has changed as time goes on is my breadth of interest. When I was younger, I tended to be pretty selective about what I liked. As I got older, I saw the beauty in many more things. I remember that I used to hate Gaudí's buildings, but now I see the aesthetic point of his wild, quirky structures.

Who and what inspires you now?

MARK BOND

I am constantly looking and the archive I carry round in my head gets fuller and fuller; every day brings something new. Inspirations certainly change as life goes on and new materials or techniques can often lead to new design solutions. It's the job of every designer working in the consumer market to keep their finger on the pulse of what is happening in their particular area of interest and the world in general. I'm often inspired by objects and artefacts I find in flea markets and junk shops; similarly I find visits to museums, especially those in other countries, very thought-provoking. I shall never forget my visit to the Whitney in New York, about twenty years ago, when I saw a huge Shaker exhibition, or indeed the archive of the Vitra Museum with all Charles Eames's early prototypes and experiments.

In no particular order, some of my favourite sources of inspiration include: geometric structures, prewar racing cars, leaf skeletons, agricultural equipment, tractor seats, physics and chemistry laboratories, early machinery and astronomical devices such as orreries, Japanese teahouses, spacecraft, tents and yurts, fishing boats, piers and bridges, propellers, old aeroplanes and anything connected with travel in the 1920s and '30s, kites, Thonet bentwood furniture, surfboards and skiffs, fireworks, deckchairs, warehouses in Amsterdam, watermills and windmills, origami, saddles, scaffolding, both metal and bamboo, geodesic domes, butterflies, moths and beetles and especially dragonflies, operating theatres, dentists' chairs and hospital trolleys, suits of armour, sculpture by Anthony Caro, Jean Arp and Alexander Calder, mandolins, cellos, clarinets and trumpets, old woodworking and gardening tools, films by Ridley Scott and Peter Greenaway . . . and much, much more.

What is the most exciting innovation you have ever seen?

JOHN SORRELL

A Stealth bomber, for its shape and technology, rather than its purpose. The Mir Space Station was pretty wonderful, too.

What's so special about the Porsche 911?

JAMIE ABBOTT

The 911 has always been my dream car. Ever since I made some money in my thirties, some thirty-five years ago, I have owned fourteen in various different colours.

The Porsche is a designer's car, both in the way that it looks and the way it is engineered. It was very austere in its early days, difficult and dangerous to drive until you

ABOVE: *The Stealth bomber: beautiful in form, horrible in function.*

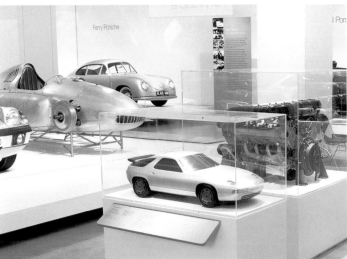

LEFT: *As a lifelong fan of the car, I took a particular interest in the informative and inspirational Porsche exhibition mounted by the Design Museum.*

mastered it. Now, I rather regret, it is much more comfortable and very much less demanding in practically every way; for example, its tiptronic gearbox makes driving easier but less fun. In a curious fashion, I seem to have kept pace with its development so that even now, at my age, it still seems a suitable car to drive. In fact, I suspect the new Porsches would feel a bit tame and over-sophisticated to a boy racer.

Why do shopping trolleys never push straight?
MURIEL GRAY

Because they have four wheels, each of which can turn in any direction it feels like. Try three wheels or shopping in a small village store.

What is the difference between (say) a well-designed table at £250 and a similar design at £1,000?
ANN INGRAM

The difference is usually to do with the quantity of tables made and the quality of the materials used. A tabletop that is finished in veneered American oak over a chipboard base will be vastly cheaper than a table made of solid English oak. They may well appear very similar in design, but the difference in quality is usually obvious, even to the undiscerning eye.

If you had to select three things – buildings, products, works of art – that you would love to have designed or put your name to, what would they be?
PATRICK LEPERCQ

1. The Citroën 2CV, commonly known as the *deux chevaux*. Then I'd like to have moved on to design the Citroën D19.
2. The Guggenheim Museum by Frank Lloyd Wright. Although it's not the perfect gallery for showing art, it is a wonderful, organic space that makes you happy to be alive.
3. I would love to have painted Rothko's later work. If I had to choose one, it would be *No. 10*, painted in the 1950s, and presented to the Museum of Modern Art in New York by Philip Johnson.

The Guggenheim Museum in New York, designed by Frank Lloyd Wright.

What is your favourite chair?

SEBASTIAN CONRAN

It's a toss-up between a Thonet bentwood café chair, an Eames soft pad and the Karuselli. If I really have to choose one, then it would be the Thonet café chair, because it epitomizes all the principles of design, manufacture and distribution that I believe in. It was designed for an unfulfilled requirement for a mass and growing market; it was economical to manufacture, using beechwood, a raw material in plentiful supply in Eastern Europe. Innovative techniques were used in its manufacture (steam bending) and it was designed so that it could be shipped all over the world in a disassembled state and put together on arrival. The chair is flexible and springy, which means that it is not only comfortable but also that it can withstand the very demanding usage of café life. It's over 150 years since it was first made and it has been in production continuously ever since – certainly the most successful chair of all time.

Thonet bentwood café chair.

What is the most elegant piece of furniture ever made?

DAVID TANG

For elegance, it's difficult to choose from the work of Hoffmann, Ruhlmann, Chareau and Eileen Gray, but in the end I think I would opt for Mackintosh's tall, ebonized ladderback chair.

Your contemporaries have described your delight in touching and feeling the shape of objects. Is touch the most important sense in evaluating an object? And from where do you think you acquired your feeling for form?

NICHOLAS IND

All sensations are important when you are judging an object. For me, I suppose, visual pleasure is the most crucial – shape, colour and visual texture. Holding the object and feeling its shape and texture is an important way of confirming this preliminary judgement (e-commerce, beware!). I don't think designers always pay enough attention to the sensuous nature of the objects they design, or notice how people hold them in different ways, feeling their curves and surfaces and even trying to extract a smell.

Charles Rennie Mackintosh's tall ladderback chair.

A huge puffball: a wonderful shape, texture and smell. Delicious sliced and fried in bacon fat.

Who knows where you acquire these responses from, but they are obviously there from birth – for most of us, our mother's bosom is our first learning curve. Awareness of different sensations also undoubtedly develops in later life. From the days when I was a potter, I can particularly remember the feeling of throwing pots, the slimy clay responding to the pressure of my fingers, and the texture of biscuit-fired pots and glazed surfaces. My bosom days are not entirely over, but perhaps I should be content with the curves of Noguchi and Brancusi.

The sense of smell is one of the strongest senses, evoking memories, thoughts and feelings that can be a powerful drive when designing. Has there been a moment in time, a memory that you've experienced connected with the sense of smell, that has inspired you to design something in particular?

JO MALONE

I am always thinking about smell when I design restaurants and cafés, wondering how to let just the right degree permeate the restaurant from the kitchen. We all know about the provocative and appetizing smell of roast coffee, baked bread, fried bacon, truffles and garlic. How about grilled porcini, roast game birds, Seville orange marmalade, spiced cakes, *beurre noisette*, pralines, gingerbread, *fonds de veau*, tarragon sauce and, best of all, damp wine cellars?

I once designed some bedroom furniture in cedar of Lebanon because I like the smell so much and because, practically speaking, it acts as a natural moth-repellent.

The smell of coffee and fresh-baked bread takes me back to my early Soup Kitchen days. We had the second espresso machine in London, and caffeine became the favourite stimulant of the 1950s in much the same way that cannabis became the favourite drug of the 1960s. My elbow used to ache after a night frothing milk on the Gaggia.

Could you discuss a design that you have worked on that matters to you and describe the process and the working method?

DEYAN SUDJIC

Pretty well all the designs that I work on matter to me. As far as the process is concerned, it depends on what it is that I am designing. A large interior, such as a restaurant, involves a whole team of people and is obviously a much more complex endeavour than a piece of furniture or a relatively simple domestic product.

I produce at least a hundred ideas for furniture every year, usually in the form of a very simple pencil drawing on layout paper, the back of a letter or memo – the proverbial 'used envelope'. I keep a large box of these sketches and go through them with our furniture buyers at regular intervals. The buyers also produce briefs that describe the products they need to expand their ranges. Merchandise meetings, when we sit down and review new products that the buyers have sourced, are also very productive as a way of stimulating ideas about new products to fill gaps.

After this process of deliberation, we decide which sketch designs we will develop further. At this stage, we have a fairly clear idea of the price target, basic dimensions and materials. I then work with my assistants to develop the design, and discuss construction and material usage in order to produce the most economical result. They generally go on to make a simple scale model that allows us to refine proportions and isolate any construction problems, and then proceed to make a full-size prototype, usually in MDF if the design is for a piece of cabinet furniture.

The prototype enables us to further discuss proportion, materials, manufacturing methods (with the help of the Benchmark team), rough cost and viability. We present it to the buyers and if they feel that it is a product that they want to proceed with, Benchmark then makes a fully finished working prototype that can be shown at a merchandising meeting for final acceptance – or not!

At this stage, and usually before the meeting, the buyers have decided which manufacturers will be asked to quote on the product. We produce detailed drawings for the manufacturers to price. Once the manufacturer is chosen, further consultation with them will take place before the product is finally put into production as they may wish to suggest constructional modifications because of their particular skills or equipment.

Because our furniture is destined for outlets all over the world, we also have to consider how the product will be packed and how it will be assembled on arrival. Packaging and assembly are therefore an integral part of the design brief.

My office in the apartment at Shad Thames.

Does the future look grim for the 6B pencil?

TINA ELLIS

6B is a little on the soft side – I'm more of a 2B man myself. Any designer must obviously embrace new technology, but must also be well grounded in crafts, because quite often it is a combination of old and new that produces the best result.

While if you reject technology out of hand, you'll certainly get left behind, I think it's now recognized that technology is no substitute for the quickness and efficiency with which brain and hand can connect and demonstrate creative ideas via pencil and paper. The problem with technology in all the multifarious forms practised in design and architectural offices is that it can become so addictive that it absorbs time and energy and crushes creativity. People become techno junkies rather than creative whizz kids. Rather than let technology gain the upper hand, designers need to allow more poetry and 2B pencils into their work.

When I look at the manuals that accompany new cars, mobile phones, laptops, audiovisual systems or even word processors, I realize that not only could I spend the rest of my life reading them, but if I really used all the 'functions' I'd need another life as well. Thank God for the 2B pencil and the A4 layout pad.

You are known for being forward-looking, but you display a keen personal reluctance to embrace anything remotely technological. You are not a Luddite, as you like to say: you installed electronic point-of-sale systems before almost anyone else; you drive a state-of-the-art motorcar; and, however vicariously, you depend on rather a lot of modern technology to make your life tick over smoothly. Yet you rant about computers, mobile phones, remote controls, compact disc players, etc. Discuss.
VICKI CONRAN

I have always believed that technology should act as our servant and work to make life easier and more pleasant; I've tried to use it in this way. However, I find that much of today's technology seems to do the reverse; it makes life more complex and wastes time. Faced with singing and dancing, multi-functioning equipment, how many people long for simple ON and OFF buttons, or to be able to understand and mend their household equipment when it goes wrong. I do.

Does technology really improve our lives? There is no doubt that the huge increase in the number of television channels has dumbed-down programmes and increasingly turned people into couch potatoes; that photocopying eliminates forests; that architects and designers who only work on CAD equipment lose the ability to communicate with speed and sensitivity. How many people surf the Internet as a placebo? How many people buy things from a dot com when they could get the same products from a shop around the corner, quicker and cheaper? The technology around us can become so absorbing in itself that there is no time left to enjoy its benefits. My principal complaint is that people seem to rush to embrace every new bit of technology as soon as it comes out before making a proper balanced assessment as to whether it will really improve the quality of their lives.

Do you own a mobile phone?
NICOLE SWENGLEY

There's one in my car but I never use it. This is an effort to keep life simple and save precious time. I think people over-communicate to an absurd degree. My wife has one.

The 'Conran style' is now classic. Do you still consider your designs innovative and ground-breaking? Do you worry about falling into the trap of becoming passé like many other fashion designers?

VITTORIO RADICE

I have never tried to produce fashionable or ground-breaking design. Obviously, any designer is affected by what's happening in the world at a particular time, but my fundamental aim throughout my life has always been to produce useful things at a price that most people can afford. I've never designed anything that has reached icon status, and I suspect I never will.

Plain, simple and useful things don't win many design prizes, but neither do they go out of fashion – think of the 'little black dress'. I'm delighted that Jasper Morrison (nephew of my ex-wife and son of my ex-secretary) is getting praise and recognition for his plain and simple approach to design. His work seems symbolic of the emergence of a British style of design, rather in the Jean Muir tradition, essentially modest and stylish without being overly fashionable or trendy.

How is it that a small country such as ours (which in general favours floral carpets, chintz sofas and net curtains) produces some of the most contemporary and innovative designs and designers in the world?

MARK BOND

One of the reasons we have so many excellent creative designers in the UK is because we have invested more than any other country in design and art schools. Incidentally, art schools have also proved something of a forcing ground for the music industry – just look at the careers of two ex-art students, John Lennon and Bryan Ferry.

The art school phenomenon was originally an offshoot of the 1851 Exhibition and the subsequent foundation of the V & A, which was supposed to restore 'art' to 'manufacture' and demonstrate that design could improve the commercial appeal of our hugely successful industries. Since the war, British manufacturing has seen a serious decline but designers have increased in number enormously. A few little cultural blips like the 'Britain Can Make It' exhibition and the 1951 Festival of Britain have also encouraged people to enter the design profession. But none of these factors alone account for the fact that London is now the creative centre of the universe and stands a good chance of remaining so. We are, by and large, a creative and practical nation and can draw on a huge cultural history. But I like to think that our creativity comes from even further back and the reality is that our Roman genes are at last getting an outing.

It's taken nearly fifty years, but 'good design' is everywhere now. Do you like what you see?
MAURICE LIBBY

The taste of this country has changed dramatically over the last thirty years or so because modern designs are at last becoming available at prices that everybody can afford. Who would have believed that IKEA, in the relatively short time that they have traded in this country, could now be the largest home furnishings retailer in the UK? If people are only offered chintzy, floral carpets and horrible net curtains, this is all they can buy and therefore it becomes their taste. Give them an alternative and they can make a choice. I am enormously encouraged by this change of taste. It now has its own momentum.

What I don't like are those contemporary designs that are more to do with fashion than conviction, the sort of 'everything has to be lime green' mentality, or those that are poor pastiches of original ideas. Integrity is very visible. I think that Gap's success owes much to the fact that its designs have total integrity and are not the work of copyists knocking off a high-street version of what's previously been seen on the catwalk.

There's no doubt that, thanks to you, the tastes and expectations of consumers have been raised considerably over the past decades. However, the world of design (and food) could also be seen as becoming a victim of its own success. Do you find this irritating, disturbing or a small price to pay for the overall rise in the understanding and acceptance of 'good design' as an essential part of life?
BRIDGET BODOANO

Generally I am delighted to have seen a huge shift in the public's appreciation of design during my working life and it's always flattering to be credited with having been involved (with many others) in this change. I've always found it difficult to accept second best or a compromise but I have learned that something is better than nothing and therefore I'm reasonably happy to see things that have attempted the change but not quite made it. The second or third time around they may get it right. The effort to make a change is the most important thing.

Unfortunately, there are many examples of thoughtless attempts to jump on the bandwagon made by people who don't really care and only want to make money. And as you go around trade fairs or visit provincial restaurants, you also see endless examples of businesses who've paid lip service to change but have simply muddled through and missed the point. There seems to be a hesitation among many small businesses to work with designers or creative chefs because they believe it is a cost they can avoid. They seem happy, however, to pay the fees of qualified lawyers and accountants. I would have thought that it is obvious that the product you offer for sale must come at the top of your list of priorities as it makes the difference between success and failure.

As a pioneer you have often been copied. Does imitation flatter you or do you find it irritating?

PAULA PRYKE

If it is blatant copying for monetary gain, it is extremely irritating. On the other hand, it seems to me that different people around the world often have much the same idea at the same moment in time. When this happens, everybody should be relaxed and understanding. Very few ideas are truly original, but are usually the development of something that has been seen somewhere, sometime.

ANNA FORD:
Is good design a civilizing influence?

If you believe the Romans civilized Britain, which I do, then good design certainly has had a civilizing influence. The Romans brought with them a style of architecture, design and engineering far in advance of the wattle-and-daub huts of our forebears. In the eighteenth century, an appreciation for well-designed buildings, furniture and everyday objects such as glassware and knives and forks were similarly part of what it was to be an educated and cultivated person. If you look at recent achievements in architecture and design, you can see that we are more optimistic about the future and don't constantly have to trawl back through the past to comfort ourselves. I was given a pamphlet the other day, issued by the Greenwich Conservatives, that described the Tory home as one that was furnished with solid, traditional pieces, whereas New Labour's had bright, modern and colourful furniture from The Conran Shop. I must say, I took it rather as a compliment. I think a civilized society is one that has the confidence to live in the present, to learn from history rather than repeat it.

In this context, I remember when my design group was asked to design offices for Lord Gowrie, then minister for the arts. Our contemporary scheme attracted a huge degree of criticism, not least because it was perceived as an extravagance. In fact, it cost considerably less than the average ministerial office refit, with antique partner's desk and handblocked wallpaper and certainly a fraction of what was later spent by Derry Irvine. The criticism of our scheme was really directed at the style; the cost issue was just a camouflage.

Can an obsession with design detract from good human relations?

In their work, designers neglect human relations at their peril. I believe that a designer or architect is, to an extent, a servant. You always have to think how your work will improve the

Our open-plan apartment above the office in London, photographed in 1999. The building where our offices are located was designed by Michael Hopkins and built by David Mellor.

quality of life of your customers, which means you have to place yourself in their shoes. When you are working directly for someone, it's often a balancing act between satisfying your own principles and pleasing the client.

It's true that many passionate and obsessive designers often seem to be shut in their own world, as if they suffered from Asperger's syndrome. Design does take a high degree of dedication, which can mean that there is little left over to give, but this is equally true of any absorbing career. The difficulty with designers, of course, is often in their domestic arrangements. I imagine that it would be difficult to share your life with someone like John Pawson, for example, whose house expresses his very strong design philosophy, unless you went along with those views yourself.

Designers are often criticized for being 'Style Nazis', fussing over details that don't bother other people. But in some ways it is perfectly understandable. You could imagine a classical musician, who was devoted to Mozart, finding it difficult to put up with a partner's taste in Muzak. The problem with design is that it touches so many aspects of our lives, from the car we drive to the toaster, that there are potentially many more areas of conflict than you can predict at the start of a relationship.

It can also be somewhat dismaying for a designer, who identifies strongly with his or her work, when a partner does not share the same enthusiasms. When our children had finally all left home, vacating the top floor at Barton Court, Caroline and I discussed how to refurbish it. I suggested that she might like to have a go doing it up herself; she'd always expressed an interest in this area and I imagined that she might enjoy it. The next thing I knew there were four Mercedes shooting brakes in the drive and a team of interior designers were busily creating an execrable scheme at vast expense. It upset me because the result was so totally at odds with what I'd thought she'd always believed in – our tastes had always seemed to coincide in other areas – and because I had imagined that she would have enjoyed the opportunity to create something herself rather than bringing in other people to do it for her.

Did you ever consider teaching or giving masterclasses? What advice would you give to a fourteen-year-old wanting to make a career in design?
STAFFORD CLIFF

Back in the late 1950s I did teach evening classes at the Central School. My star pupil was Min Hogg, who later became the founding editor of *World of Interiors*. Later, I also taught for a while at the Royal College of Art. I must admit that these were less than rewarding experiences because both schools were badly organized at that time and you never knew if the students would turn up. Usually they didn't, which maybe says something about me as a teacher.

I'd advise any young would-be designer to absorb knowledge left, right and centre: visit design fairs, exhibitions and schools, read books and magazines about design, arrange to do work experience in designers' offices and to talk to as many designers as possible. I'd also suggest that they spend some time learning a craft or several crafts in an area that interests them; understanding how things are actually made and how different materials shape the design process is fundamental to good design practice.

What are the ingredients for a good book? What is more important: pictures, layout or text?

GHISLAINE BAVOILLOT

We are both involved with what are called 'illustrated books', a term that is often used with some disparagement. All three elements you mention have a role to play in making a good book, the pictures and layout to convey clarity of vision, the text to be informative and stimulate the imagination, but it is a question of achieving the right balance. My preferences are for clear layout and legible type so that the pictures do not subsume the words. Most of my battles with graphic designers, which I don't always win, concern this issue.

How do you convey your design vision in the books that you publish? What do you look for when buying a book?

CAROLINE PROUD

My first major book was *The House Book*, published twenty-eight years ago. It started life as a training manual for Habitat staff, grew and grew, and ended up as a bestseller around the world. Most of my books have been based on putting ideas and options in front of people so they can make their own decisions. Over the years, I have enjoyed working with various editors, graphic designers and picture researchers and the whole process has been a training exercise for me, allowing me to see and read a lot of information that I might not otherwise have come across. When I'm putting together a book, I look at thousands of images and select the ones that fit my vision. I might also crop them down – a bit of a cheat!

I love to handle a well-made book, beautifully printed on good paper, with the type set in such a way that it's a pleasure to read, but I also like the original Penguin paperbacks and admired their ability to get good books into people's hands at a price that anybody could afford. And I love bookshops. My favourite bookshop in London is John Sandoe near Sloane Square, which seems to epitomize everything a good bookshop should be.

Unfortunately, I don't have a lot of time to read during the working week; I hate to start a book one minute and put it down the next. For this reason, I do most of my reading on holiday – design and architecture books, thrillers, books like *Captain Corelli's Mandolin*, *Bonfire of the Vanities* or even *War and Peace*.

The first House Book, which began as an in-house training manual, broke many of the conventions of illustrated book design but became a huge international success, selling over 2¼ million copies.

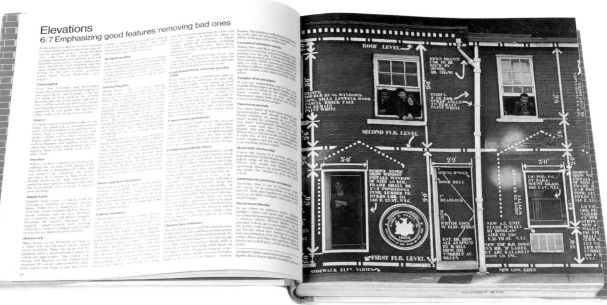

In the postwar years of reconstruction, there was a profound belief within the design community in the social and ethical importance of design. Good design would help to lead to good citizenship. Terence, you were an important part of that. In the light of the design 'gold rush' of the 1980s and 1990s – when ethics went seriously out of fashion – how do you look back on those years? Do you still hold to your original beliefs? Or is 'good' design just about the bottom line?

CHRISTOPHER FRAYLING

I have always believed that 'intelligent' (as I prefer to call it, rather than 'good') design could help to improve the quality of people's lives. I was lucky to be a student in the immediate postwar years, when the Welfare State was introduced; we were inspired both by these democratic changes and by the teachings of William Morris and the Bauhaus.

The 'creative industries' have obviously changed out of all recognition in the last fifty years, but then so have the opportunities. The increase in commercial success has led to a situation where design is big business; in the process it has lost much of its crusading spirit. I suppose I can bear a little responsibility for that. When designers like myself demonstrate that we can be financially successful, it inevitably encourages others to set up in business with moneymaking as their prime objective. Many were similarly encouraged by the general 'greed is good' ethos of the Thatcher years. This trend has undoubtedly damaged the image of the profession and resulted in some remarkably shoddy work, although the recession of the early 1990s did weed out the ranks somewhat.

My beliefs have not changed. I am still passionately convinced that intelligent design is of fundamental importance, not only to the economic survival of Britain, but also in terms of improving the quality of everyday life for ordinary people. Obviously, any business has to trade at a profit to succeed under our economic system, but a company that allows the bottom line to become its *raison d'être* is unlikely to stay in business for very long.

I had hoped that the present government's initial recognition of the importance of the creative industries might have developed into a proper strategy. I suspect, however, that the ridiculous and never-ending criticism that has been slung at the Dome has made them shy to champion the cause of creativity as something that is both socially and ethically important.

Education, in many ways, holds the key; an educated consumer is the best way to improve the quality of what is designed and made. When I made some real money in the early 1980s, I set up the Conran Foundation. This is an educational charity that has been almost entirely devoted to the establishment and year-to-year funding of first the Boilerhouse project at the V & A some twenty years ago, and subsequently the Design Museum at Butlers Wharf, which was launched twelve years ago. These two enterprises, I hope, have helped to educate the public, particularly schoolchildren, and make them aware of the importance of design in everyone's life so that they could make informed judgements about the things they would buy.

Margaret Thatcher opened the Design Museum at Butlers Wharf with great enthusiasm. However, she was disgusted to discover that many of the things we exhibited were not made in Britain, and said so.

You have had an immense influence on the fabric of modern Britain. Does the attitude in this country disillusion you and how do you feel about that?

OLIVER PEYTON

During my life I've seen people's attitudes to design and food change to such an extent it would seem churlish to be disillusioned. Frustrated, perhaps, that so many battles have to be fought and so much bureaucracy has to be overcome to make things happen. I feel particularly sad that the Labour government, who seemed to recognize the importance of creativity when they were first elected, have gone on to do very little to encourage it after their initial burst of enthusiasm.

DEYAN SUDJIC:

How important was your relationship with Paul Reilly?

Paul Reilly was a great supporter of 'design for the people'. I suppose I was a little disappointed with his very Scandinavian Arts and Crafts approach, but he was charged by government to persuade industry that design was an integral part of success, so the Scandinavian example was a useful touchstone for him to use. The Design Council was a vibrant place under his leadership. He was extraordinarily able politically and was a kind, knowledgeable and witty man. He did a wonderful job as chairman in launching my Foundation when it started the Boilerhouse at the V & A and then moved to the Design Museum at Butlers Wharf. We miss him.

What made you create the Design Museum? What happened at the V & A that triggered the move to Butlers Wharf? And what made Stephen Bayley resign?

When I was a student, I spent a great deal of time in museums, especially the V & A. The history of design in the decorative arts and in all types of scientific and engineering products is enormously well documented in this country, but my fellow students and I were continually frustrated that we could see nothing contemporary. We felt that we were in a country that only cared about its glorious past and was extremely uninterested in the present and the future. It was only when I went to the Triennales in Milan that I realized how stimulating and influential it was for both students and manufacturers to see the design of the best contemporary products in the world.

I started to dream about how something similar could happen in the UK; when I made some money on the flotation of Habitat in 1980, I set up the Conran Foundation with the idea of creating a permanent home for the display of modern design. I talked to Paul Reilly about it and he introduced me to Stephen Bayley, who became its first director. We then met up with Roy Strong at the V & A, who offered us a squalid, dingy space of about four hundred square metres in the basement of the museum, which had been the old boiler room.

That was the start of the Boilerhouse project. We converted the space into a simple white rectangle and during our five years at the V & A put on about twenty-five different exhibitions; one of the last was 'Coca-Cola: The Making of a Brand'.

Our difficulties at the V & A paradoxically arose out of our success. Some of our exhibitions attracted more visitors than the rest of the V & A put together. Ironically, at a time when the museum was busily marketing itself as 'an ace caff with quite a nice museum attached', there was also unease about the perceived commercialism of our exhibitions. Matters came to a head; the curators and keepers got up in arms and stormed Roy Strong's office demanding that the Boilerhouse project should be ejected from the museum. Roy became very flustered and told us that our five-year lease would not be renewed. As I write this, I note that the current exhibition at the V & A is about branding!

I decided to move our activities to a site I was developing at Butlers Wharf, near Tower Bridge, and this is where we built the Design Museum. Stephen was involved in planning and opening the museum and played a major role in publicizing its launch (at that time it was the first of its kind in the world). However, it soon became clear that the administration of the museum and its finances were not something he relished; what also became clear was that the brands about which he was so enthusiastic included himself. As they say, it was decided that he should leave to 'pursue other interests', which indeed he has done to great effect.

You have given more money to the arts than virtually anyone in the UK. But no one knows about this. You gave in excess of £20 million to create the Design Museum, but it does not bear your name. Are you that modest, or simply not very good at your own PR?
COLIN TWEEDY

Although I am very proud of what my gift has achieved at the Design Museum it would be wrong to boast about it, as it is only part of the money that is and has been required to fund the museum and its activities.

When the museum was established in 1989, Margaret Thatcher welcomed it as a new funding model for arts-based institutions. She said that a third of the money should come from private sponsorship, a third as a result of the institution's own efforts (ticket and shop sales, for example) and a third from government. Government, unfortunately, has never delivered its third. Over the next three years we will receive £200,000 per annum from the Department of Culture, Media and Sport; nothing like a third, but very much better than nothing.

LEFT: *The derelict building at Butlers Wharf* (ABOVE) *converted by our architects into the Design Museum* (BELOW). *Prince Charles, when he saw the model, took objection to the flat roof.*

RIGHT: *The Verner Panton exhibition at the Design Museum, designed by Tom Dixon.*

With an increasing number of visitor attractions and fierce competition for funding and sponsorship, how do you believe the Design Museum can differentiate itself so that it is still prospering in another ten years' time?

NICHOLAS BULL

The Design Museum is unique in Britain, and it remains one of the few public museums wholly dedicated to design in the world. We specialize in those subjects that touch everybody's life, from exhibitions of ordinary household products to futuristic visions of the city. In the years to come, we are going to have to do an even better job of demonstrating to the public at large, and the government in particular, the importance of intelligent design to both the consumer and the national economy.

All the fine arts – theatre, ballet, opera, music, literature and poetry – are exceedingly important in a civilized society. But the truth of the matter is that many of these cultural activities directly interest only a tiny proportion of the public. Although there is constant quibbling about the level of arts subsidies from government, sponsorship or the Lottery, quite substantial sums have been forthcoming in recent years. The other creative industries, such as design, architecture, photography and fashion, for example, receive the square root of practically nothing. Yet these are the very 'arts' that have a real impact on people's lives. They are also vital for the economic health of the country.

There appears to be a common perception that creative industries should be able to finance their own activities, simply because they are industries. As you have seen at the Design Museum, this is simply not the case. Even on an individual level, I could name far more wealthy actors and musicians than architects and designers. You are right that it is a constant slog to get sponsorship and support; the small grant that we will receive from the DCMS over the next three years represents a significant recognition of this difficulty. Let's hope it doesn't get squandered on bureaucracy.

In the future, I would like to see the Design Museum become more self-sufficient so that the Foundation can devote some of its income to educating young designers, chefs and craftspeople in modern manufacturing techniques. In this country, there remains a gulf between theory and practice that has been a contributing factor in the loss of some of our most talented young designers, who are forced to work abroad for foreign manufacturers. I would also like the museum to build a collection of modern, intelligently designed products, which again could be used for educational purposes.

My long-term ambition is to persuade the government or Lottery to fund a public space where all the creative industries could get together in one venue; somewhere just as impressive as Tate Modern, where stimulating exhibitions and displays across a wide range of disciplines could take place. When that happens, the importance of design will finally be properly appreciated and London will truly be perceived as the creative capital of the world.

Design is, more than ever, at the crossroads of economics, politics and culture. Yet design is still treated and displayed by most design museums or by museums' design departments as a sub-chapter of art history and a showcase for good-looking objects. How can the Design Museum bring a new vision to challenge researchers and curators?

FRANÇOISE JOLLANT KNEEBONE

I have always hoped that the Design Museum would find a way of demonstrating to ordinary people, especially those who are not particularly interested in art, design or museums, that intelligent design of their homes, offices, transport and the products they use, could make a significant difference to the quality and enjoyment of their lives. The work that the museum does with schools helps this process, but it is an insidious influence rather than a dramatic one and I believe more drama is needed. I believe our new director, Alice Rawsthorn, will bring this sense of drama to the museum.

You have had a number of careers, as designer, property developer, retailer and restaurateur to name but a few; you have been a risk-taker and experienced more variety than all but a very privileged few – but inevitably, both ups and downs. A while ago, probably in your fifties, you told me that people were more content in their even-numbered decades and more anxious in their odd-numbered ones. As you begin an odd-numbered decade, what do you want to do (and feel you have not done) before you reach eighty; why haven't you done it before, and how are you going to avoid the anxieties?

ANTHONY SALZ

I'd like to persuade the government that intelligent design is of fundamental importance, not only to the economic prosperity of our country, but also to the quality of life for its people. I've tried to do so before, but it's a long hard slog, difficult in a country that abounds with traditionalists who don't want to face up to the present, let alone the future. But I think things are finally moving in the right direction. As far as anxieties are concerned, I'm afraid I've never been able to avoid them and I suspect I never will. If you're totally self-satisfied, you might be able to be anxiety-free, but most creative people aren't by nature complacent.

You clearly like to live in an environment in which you create a harmony and tension between well-designed manufactured objects and traditional craft objects. What place does art occupy in your life? Many of your friends are artists. Do you collect their work?

NICHOLAS SEROTA

Art has always played quite a major part in my life. Because I like them both as friends and artists, I have collected and been given work by Richard Smith, Howard Hodgkin, David Hockney, Patrick Caulfield, Allen Jones, Tony Caro, Eduardo Paolozzi, Francis Bacon, Stephen Buckley, Dennis Wirth Miller and many others. Because they are or have been friends, their work means more to me than pieces I have bought from artists I have never met.

What I dislike is art bought purely for investment, or as a symbol of aesthetic or intellectual elitism. For many wealthy collectors, art is simply a physical, demonstrable manifestation of their success. What I find equally dismaying are those who acquire beautiful pieces of art but then appear to be utterly indifferent to other aspects of their immediate environment. It seems to me that good art and intelligent design are utterly interwoven and that if you appreciate one there is no reason why you should not appreciate the other. The people I admire most are those who don't compartmentalize different aspects of life, but care just as much about the design of a car or a piece of furniture, or about a book, a restaurant meal or a suit, as they do a work of art.

Why have you not assembled over the years one of the foremost collections of post-1960s painting and sculpture?

RICHARD SMITH

I think I have the largest collection of your work of anybody I know. I also have a large number of works by many other contemporary artists, some of whom are listed above. In many instances, such works are displayed in our various restaurants and offices and on the whole they are prints rather than grand paintings. This is because I don't want to live surrounded by security devices and because I think that great and valuable works of art deserve a public space. I've never seen myself as a serious art collector, only as someone who likes to surround himself with things that he likes.

Although painting and sculpture have played an important part in your life it seems that little is known of this enthusiasm and patronage. Can you name particular favourites among artists (or their work)?

DAVID CHALONER

My most daft bit of patronage was in the early 1970s when I started a gallery in Covent Garden in a wonderful space called Garage, to show the work of young artists who couldn't get a look-in at Cork Street galleries. I asked Kasmin, David Hockney, Tony Caro, Peter Blake and the gallery director Martin Attwood to decide who we would show.

They all found it very difficult to decide; I remember David Hockney suggesting in total exasperation that we should show the drawings of Michelangelo. We did have some critically successful shows, including one by a girl who collected all the things she found in her bed and framed them very neatly. I am sure she must have gone on to be exhibited by Charles Saatchi. I lost a lot of money and became a bit depressed by the constant disagreements. When the gallery closed after about two years Tony Caro gave me a piece of his sculpture as a thank you for my efforts and that made it all worthwhile.

The most interesting experience for me is to commission an artist to produce an original piece for a restaurant, office or whatever, and work with them from brief to installation. The eight specially commissioned columns at Quaglino's and Allen Jones's work at Mezzo were thrilling projects. One of the greatest successes in this context is Tom Heatherwick's huge pasta-like sculpture, which oozes from the joints of the huge granite wall at Guastavino's.

As far as my favourite artist is concerned, I think Picasso comes up trumps because he was so immensely creative in so many different ways and continued to be so right up to the end of his long life. That's certainly an inspiration to me.

I've always wanted to know more about your confrontation with Howard Hodgkin in the art room at school and – perhaps connectedly – the origin of your rather envious (or grudging) attitude to 'creative' or 'star' or just gallery artists and the art world in general, the prices, the reputations, the glamour. I suppose I am asking if there is a frustrated or superseded artist somewhere in your own past.

KASMIN

I really don't remember having any confrontation with Howard at Bryanston, but I do recall that he was always immensely knowledgeable about many areas of design that particularly interested me.

We did have one rather unfortunate confrontation. I had asked him to dinner at Bibendum. When he arrived he was full of how he had been asked to school the then newly wed Duchess of York (Fergie to you and me) in the fine arts, as apparently she was set to

David Hockney's favourite meal.

Beluga Caviare

Watercress Soup   Truite au bleu

Châteaubriands Sauce Béarnaise

Mange tout   haricots vert

Cheese

Creme Brulée

no coffee (it is a killer)

Gewertzkraminer
Château Lafitte
Château Yquem.

*David Hockney's menu for the Neal Street Restaurant, circa 1971. The original, which lists
his own favourite dishes, specifies: 'No coffee — it's a killer'. It still hangs in the restaurant.*

*Tom Heatherwick's plywood gazebo, made for his degree show at the Royal College of Art,
now sits in my garden. It's a perfect place to sit and smoke a cigar.*

take the 'royal' interest in them. I asked him if he wouldn't prefer to help students at the Royal College of Art; as a council member I knew that his influence would have been very welcome at that particular time. He thought that this was the most insulting thing that anyone had ever suggested to him. Why should he give his valuable time to a bunch of art students? With that, he got up and walked out, leaving his half-eaten supper behind.

Over the years, I have always been a bit bemused by the amount of attention paid to fine artists and their works, in comparison to the comparative lack of recognition that the achievements of architects and designers receive. Although the situation is now changing to some extent, there is still nothing that matches the hoo-ha that surrounds the Turner Prize, or Damien's latest gimmick, or Tracey's latest unmade bed. I thought Damien's exhibition in New York was fantastic, but is he as important in the scheme of things as people like Buckminster Fuller or Norman Foster, people who really do shape the world around us?

Oscar Wilde said, 'All art is quite useless'. Would you agree?
NED CONRAN

Not at all. Art promotes sensations and fires the imagination in all sorts of useful ways.

What in your view is the difference between design and architecture?
JAMES SOANE

I really don't believe that there is a significant degree of difference; there are plenty of areas of overlap. This, however, is not necessarily borne out in the way the two disciplines are viewed. In the past, architects seemed to find it necessary to ring-fence their profession and certainly seemed to see themselves as superior beings, with designers definitely being below the salt.

In fact, many architects have convincingly demonstrated that they are good furniture or product designers, and designers have also shown that they can be quite good at designing buildings when given the opportunity – look at Charles Eames, for instance. If you consider the work of many contemporary architects, such as Nicholas Grimshaw, Norman Foster or Richard Rogers, I think you will see more evidence of the skill of an industrial designer-cum-engineer than that of a traditional architect.

Our 'Jolly Green Giant', the warehouse at Wallingford, Oxfordshire, designed by Ahrends, Burton & Koralek. The green colour was inspired by the colour of my Porsche.

The *Guardian* critic Nancy Banks-Smith once wrote: 'In my experience, if you have to keep the lavatory door shut by extending your left leg, it's modern architecture.' How would you define modern architecture?

MAGGIE HEANEY

The best is charming, exciting, sometimes technologically advanced, practical and, above all, lifts the spirits. The worst, and there is plenty of it, is exactly the reverse.

What is the most beautiful building ever built? What is the most functional?

DAVID TANG

Ronchamp by Le Corbusier, for beauty; the Seagram Building by Mies van der Rohe, for function. I also like the Penguin Pool at London Zoo by Lubetkin, the Eiffel Tower, the Jantar Mantar near Jaipur and (from what I have seen of them in film and photographs) Santiago Calatrava's new buildings in Valencia.

I love the organic, sculptural curves of Le Corbusier's Chapel of Notre Dame du Haut, Ronchamp, Haute-Saône (1950–5).

Another favourite: the supreme rationality of Mies van der Rohe's Seagram Building, New York (1956–7).

You've worked with a lot of architects throughout your career, bringing your projects to life. Who have you really enjoyed working with and who have you had the best battles with?

PAUL ZARA

Any decent architect has pretty firm ideas and deviates from them with extreme reluctance. When problems arise it is often because the client has not agreed a brief with their architect, not spent enough time discussing the brief, or both. A real understanding is vital before the architect puts pencil to paper or mouse to mat.

My first experience of working with architects was when the LCC's architects department designed our furniture factory in Thetford, Norfolk. This was a huge success, very economical, very simple and delivered on time to budget. Its extension, a large timber shed by YRM, was less successful as it didn't have any natural light. YRM's response to my complaint, 'Well, you didn't ask for it', was correct, but pretty irritating!

Richard Burton from Ahrends, Burton & Koralek was a huge pleasure to work with when we built our 'Jolly Green Giant' at Wallingford, a development that comprised offices, a showroom and a huge warehouse for Habitat. We had a close relationship and an outstanding technically advanced building was the outcome. When Richard first presented the plans for the building to me, we still hadn't decided on the colour. Then he spotted my Porsche in the street and suggested we paint the warehouse the same shade of green (without realizing that the car was mine). A week or so later, I drove into a bollard and dented the car, so I sent the damaged wing to Richard as a colour sample.

In 1966 our design group landed our largest job to date when we were asked to design the interior of Terminal One at Heathrow for BAA. The architects of the building, Frederick Gibberd & Partners, were a bit put out, since it was a job that they had hoped to do. We didn't much like their architecture and they, I suspect, didn't much like our interior, which was very robust and functional. We both behaved in quite a gentlemanly way and never criticized each other in public. Somehow the completed building worked well.

The North Terminal at Gatwick was a far happier situation. Our designers and YRM talked the same language and together we produced what was praised as a seamless building. Well, it *was* seamless until BAA's commercial department turned it from an air terminal where passengers could wait comfortably and calmly for their planes into an extremely vulgar shopping centre, filled to the brim with every sort of high-street junk you can imagine and quite a lot you can't.

You have been successful in so many fields. Is there something else you wish you had done?

JEFFREY ARCHER

Designed and built housing that was relevant to the time in which we live – housing that was intelligent, beautiful and affordable, and which in years to come people would admire in much the same way they admire Georgian houses and terraces today.

If you had to build an ideal home for the next generation, what would it be like, and where would you see it?

NORMAN FOSTER

Although the digital age allows us to be in contact with anybody, anywhere and at any time, I do think the next generation will feel the need for human contact even more than we do. So I would choose a site in a busy metropolis, preferably with a view over water and construct a tallish building with huge balconies and lots of simple undivided space for people to subdivide as they wish. Plain, tough, rather Corbusian, with a bit of Barragán-ish charm and colour and a Grimshaw-like Eden as a public space on and below the ground.

Over the years I have been involved in various discussions with government bodies, and urban design and architectural groups, on the subject of how to raise the standards of our appalling private house building; I frequently find myself quoting how you, personally and independently, have significantly contributed to transforming the restaurant and food culture of Britain from a similarly very low base. I have argued that there is little that government initiatives, particularly through town-planning processes, can achieve. It is only effectively applied cultural leadership that supplies a better product, together with increased expectations and discernment of the consumer, that will create the revolution that is needed in the taste and quality of private house building.

How would you go about things if you were to become a major house builder or be an adviser to one?

TERRY FARRELL

I would thoroughly brief the best architects, technicians and designers and ensure that they understood both the type of housing that was required and were able to work within what would undoubtedly be demanding financial constraints. I would then build several groups of houses in different areas for different income groups. One source of reference and

Hope for the future? The Foster-designed Underground station at Canary Wharf, one of the Jubilee line's wonderful new stations.

inspiration might well be the excellent Span developments initiated by Eric Lyons in the 1960s. These communities of contemporary middle-income housing have matured very well over the decades, not least because of sensitive layout and landscaping; the houses themselves still look far more modern than the average new-build today.

The next step would be to persuade mortgage lenders that these houses had a good resale value so that competitively priced mortgages were readily available. Then I would brainwash local estate agents, thereby ridding them of their preferences for half-timbered neo-Georgian tacky little boxes smothered in carriage lamps. How? Oh God, I don't know. Perhaps I could make a start by asking them if they wouldn't prefer to drive to work in a horse and trap rather than a new BMW. Or perhaps they might prefer a wind-up gramophone to a CD player. This might start some sort of thought process in their poor retrofit brains.

I would organize a huge publicity campaign, both nationally and locally, in the press, and on TV and radio. The architectural and design press would highlight the technological advances of the designs; interiors magazines would feature houses that were completed and lived in. Rumours would spread that all the Spice Girls had bought one; the Beckhams, one each; and that the Blairs, Prescotts and Browns had each reserved a house for their retirement. The main thrust of the publicity would be to make people proud and excited to be living in a house that was designed for life today – and to make them ashamed even to consider buying a mean little repro box.

If such houses lived up to their promise and were affordable, I really do believe that a housing revolution could be started in this country. After all, it has started in practically every other area of consumer goods.

You have often expressed frustration at the many issues that protract design projects nowadays. What do you think has changed over the years to cause this and what do you think could be done to address the problems?

RICHARD DOONE

Every architect and designer knows the myriad regulations that have to be observed in the design and construction of a new building or the alteration of an old one. Some of the rules are entirely sensible and make for better, safer and more practical buildings. Many seem simply designed to encourage mediocrity. This is particularly the case when it comes to the escalating power of the planners and especially certain heritage officers, who seem to believe that it is they who should be empowered to make aesthetic judgements, not the architects. They always have time and bureaucracy on their side: should you be foolish enough to appeal against their decision, months or even years may lapse before a final decision is made. Planners seem to realize that you will probably be forced into accepting their direction because the delay will make the project unviable or the client will get cold feet and force a compromise.

Perhaps the most ridiculous situations occur when officers from different branches of the same planning department, for example fire officers and health and safety inspectors, issue conflicting instructions that they refuse to resolve between themselves, leaving the designer stranded.

It seems to me that the situation has become so complex and so absurd that the government, through the Department of the Environment, must rewrite the rules, simplifying them substantially and abandoning several hundred miles of red tape at the same time. This would be welcomed by everyone involved, not least by the planners themselves whose jobs have become so complex that in many parts of Britain they are unable to even look at the applications for months because they have such a backlog.

But in this context, my main concern is how to encourage finer and more imaginative architecture. Unfortunately, the planning process usually has the very reverse effect, dumbing down innovative schemes to such an extent that clients lose heart and simply agree to compromise because they need to get something built to keep the wheels of commerce turning. I believe this is quite a deep malaise that needs urgent action.

Given the proliferation of so many British architects who have achieved international renown over the past thirty years or so, how is it that Britain, and London in particular, has failed so abysmally to embrace their work, preferring either the neo-classical or the utilitarian?

MICHAEL GRADE

As I've already said, I think that planners in this country have an absurd amount of control over the appearance of our buildings and often stand in the way of adventurous contemporary design. Couple this with some pretty unimaginative developers and institutional investors, add in estate agents whose idea of good taste is a suburban golf club, and it is surprising that we have any decent buildings at all.

This innate conservatism was only encouraged by Prince Charles some twenty years ago, when he made it clear that he preferred a sort of repro façadism to any design that actually reflected the time we live in. When we showed our model for the Design Museum to him, he particularly disliked the flat roof; I was reminded of this later when we came to put on an exhibition about the Bauhaus. The Nazis, who were very keen to abolish the Bauhaus, also disliked flat roofs. Their reason was that 'flat roofs came from Arabia and were therefore degenerate'. Not, of course, that Prince Charles would ever have made *that* connection.

Although house building has some considerable way to go, in recent years there have been some very visible signs, in London and elsewhere, that things are at last changing. In part this has been due to some surprisingly bold decisions by companies such as Lloyd's, Channel 4 and ITN to commission modern architects to design their buildings. The advent of the Lottery has also brought some remarkable architecture to all parts of Britain; the south bank of the Thames in particular. Now that people have had the chance to see what our world-renowned architects can achieve in their own country and in their own capital city, I hope that there will be no going back to the compromised, cynical approach to building that was such a feature of the 1980s.

Did you visit the Dome and, if so, what did you think?

MARK BOND

Yes, I visited the Dome on the very first day it was open to the public. I thought it was a very beautiful structure, with the most amazing tube stations en route. Unfortunately, the content was extremely variable, with some quite excellent areas, some reasonable ones and a few that were quite awful – rather like life! I was amused by some of the strolling players or street performers who entertained the crowds; that seemed to be a charming touch. The signage I thought very poor.

My experience working on the wonderful Festival of Britain taught me the importance of having a creative supremo overseeing the direction of such large and ambitious projects. Hugh Casson performed this role admirably in 1951. I said as much to Jennie Page, the chief executive of NMEC, when she asked me for a reference for Stephen Bayley. I told her that Stephen was full of wonderful ideas but had the temperament of a hummingbird moth on LSD and was the worst administrator in a long line of worst administrators that I had ever met. Nevertheless, he got the job. Jennie later phoned me and apologized for not listening to my advice: right ideas, wrong person for the job.

Stephen's departure from the Dome fuelled the great media bonanza and took the criticism to new vitriolic levels. If every word written or spoken about the Dome had generated five pence and every picture five pounds, the Dome would have been the greatest financial success of all time. But the effect of this hugely negative reporting had the predictable impact on attendance, which ended up being less than half the projected figure for the year. Those who did go usually seemed to enjoy it; I heard schoolchildren say they learned more in one day at the Dome than in a whole term at school.

Overall, I think the Dome was really a case of far too many sous chefs stirring the broth, with no head chef to give clear instructions about technique, contents or taste. However, we are left with a very nice soup plate on what was once a rubbish tip.

When you start a new project, such as hotel or restaurant, do you always consider flowers in the design? Would you always choose garden flowers over commercial flowers? What do you consider to be your flower classics?

PAULA PRYKE

I always want fresh flowers in every interior I design. I may know from the outset where I want them and what type they should be, but usually I choose the flowers after I have completed the design. Although I always prefer garden flowers, unfortunately they don't last long in commercial environments. My personal favourites are full-blown, rather blowsy roses, sweet peas and the first hyacinths when they are greenish-blue, but best of all wild meadow flowers in early summer.

JONATHAN CHIDSEY:

Have you ever considered designing and building a permanent structure in the grounds of your home at Barton Court with the intent of leaving behind a permanent reminder of your years there?

I've often thought of building a summerhouse, rather like a Japanese teahouse crossed with the Eames house, but I know I would never get planning permission. Instead, I am more than content with my Thomas Heatherwick 'gazebo'-cum-cigar smoker's refuge.

Using the produce grown in the Barton Court garden, what would you prepare for your last meal?

A large plate of asparagus with warm butter; an *omelette aux fines herbes*, made with eggs from the hens and herbs from your beds, together with a dish of the first tiny broad beans. Raspberries and wild strawberries to follow.

What are the most important aspects of owning an outside space? Would you feel that it was important to turn this space into a garden? How would you consider a garden to differ from an inside living space?

DAN PEARSON

Like you, I find owning and tending an outdoor space one of the most important and pleasurable things in life. Over the years, I have had some tiny back gardens in London and some large ones in Suffolk, Berkshire and Provence. Whatever the scale, they have all seemed an essential component to leading a balanced life. The whole growing process and the seasonal changes that occur in a garden are an enormous pleasure to me and are as aesthetically satisfying as what is on display in any art gallery. When I sit in the garden on a sunny day, smoking a cigar and drinking a glass of wine, I can feel the stress and strain of life dripping away. I don't necessarily think that an outside space has to be highly cultivated. A meadow with grasses and wild flowers and a bit of a view, especially of a river or stream, is probably better than any man-made garden could ever be.

Ideally, I believe there should be no rigid frontier between the garden and the interior of the house. Many houses, where the climate is somewhat more benign than ours, manage to achieve this admirably. In my house in the country, I have tried to link the large living room on the south-facing front of the house to the York stone terrace and raised garden outside. Occasionally we have hot sunny days, which allow us to open all the windows and doors. When this happens I certainly feel that the garden and indoor space become as one. Everybody feels happy and kicks their shoes off, and living becomes easy, well *easier*.

TOP: *With Jonathan Chidsey, my gardener, in the walled vegetable garden at Barton Court.*
ABOVE: *My 'Chef's Garden' stand for the Evening Standard at Chelsea Flower Show, 1999.*

What is your philosophy regarding work and play? You used to enjoy gardening as a hobby. Why did you cease to pursue this?

TOM CONRAN

I try to combine work and play so they merge together in one pleasurable whole. Gardening, for example, is no longer purely a hobby and hasn't been since I started to write books about it (*The Essential Garden Book* with Dan Pearson, and *The Chef's Garden*) and to design gardens for exhibitions (for the Imperial War Museum and the *Evening Standard* at Chelsea Flower Show); we also grow herbs and vegetables for the restaurants at Barton Court and I've always thought I might like to be involved in creating a new type of garden centre. But, whether it's work or play, gardening remains a great pleasure.

Do you have to be an autocrat to run a creative business?

JOHN HEGARTY

While we would all wish to run our own creative businesses as democratically as possible, I'm absolutely sure that a certain amount of autocracy is necessary. After all, a creative business needs to have a house style and somebody has to be the keeper of that style and philosophy. Over the years, I've seen a number of creative businesses try to run themselves as true democracies. Inevitably, after a period of disruptive internal warfare, they have reverted to a form of autocracy; sad but true.

Autocracy on its own, however, is not the solution: simply ordering people about, saying 'do this' and 'don't do that', is not the way to build and develop a team. The question always is how to balance autocracy with teamwork, in other words how to lead an opinionated collection of talented people. I suppose the answer is that each person in the team has to admire the leader, not only for his or her achievements, but also because the leader recognizes, respects and is a good judge of their creative input.

We all know that an unfair amount of praise goes to the leader of a business and that the team that has created the success frequently gets left out in the cold and feels pretty bitter about their lack of recognition. I suspect that this is the case in most businesses, creative or not. So I think that not only do you have to try to get the balance right between leadership and teamwork, you must also make it absolutely clear that it is the team that makes your business a success.

As businesses grow, the need to control them increases, but the best creative people do not want to be controlled. Do you agree with this, and does this mean that small design and other creatively led businesses are inevitably better than large ones? Is this a constraint on how much the Conran businesses can expand in future?

DES GUNEWARDENA

I don't necessarily agree that the best creative people don't want to be controlled. It's much more a question of how the control is organized and exercised. I can think of many large design offices such as those of Foster, Grimshaw or Rogers that produce brilliant work and are full of (mainly) happy designers. One way of controlling a design business is to structure it so that teams of designers work on specific projects. As these projects come and go, the teams constantly change and develop. This is conducive to an exciting, creative atmosphere. In any type of work, there are some people that like a small company and some that like the buzz of a big company doing big projects. Designers are no different.

Is it easy to find the right people to assist you on a new project, and how do you find them?

WERNER BULLEN

The great thing about an expanding business is that you can spot and develop people within your existing organization who can become leaders in new projects. We sometimes advertise and very occasionally we use headhunters, although I dislike them on principle, what they do and the way they do it. By far the best source of new people are the ones who knock on our door because they have heard that we are an interesting business to work for.

What do you imagine it is like working for you?

JULIE RICHARDSON

Quite fun at times, hell at others. Seriously, I hope we create an atmosphere of general enthusiasm, where individuality and disciplined entrepreneurialism are encouraged and rewarded. I have only ever worked for someone else for about a year, otherwise I've always been 'the boss', but I never really think about it, I just get on with things.

How do you keep your MDs motivated . . . is it by kicking them continuously up the arse?
DAVID LOEWI

As far as I can remember, I have never offered any physical inducements, but I have made good use of memos, sometimes acerbic, at other times filled with lavish praise and with bonuses attached. I have always believed in putting criticism, advice or praise on paper as it is clear and unambiguous and can be discussed and reread several times if necessary.

Do you perceive any difference in the contribution to business by men and by women?
MARGARET DOWNES

No great difference and, when customers are mainly women, it makes great sense for a woman to run the business.

Do you feel honesty is a liability in business?
ELKIN PIANIM

The very reverse. A lack of honesty, I think, is the greatest liability in business and anybody who believes otherwise should certainly not be in business or, indeed, any other walk of public life.

AMANDA ROBINSON:
Which upsets you more, criticism of you personally or of your businesses?

Criticism of the business, as that also means criticism of me in my book!

Do you think you'll always employ a PA?

Yes, as long as I am working, which I hope will be for the rest of my life. I cannot imagine getting by without a facilitator!

Why, oh why, are you always so grumpy about holidays?

What makes me grumpy is that frequent holidays upset the smooth running of the business. How many times do you hear that a decision cannot be taken because the relevant person is away on holiday? The period from Christmas to New Year is a case in point; this year many businesses in this country will shut for over eleven days. For many companies this means that if they have been successful in the run-up to Christmas, they will lose all they have gained.

There are 8,760 hours in a year. If you calculate the average working week, the average number of holidays, bank holidays, and average days off sick, the average person only works for 1,589 hours in the year – or about eighteen per cent of their time. I suspect that work-related stress may have more to do with the stress involved in lengthy commutes to work, which given the poor state of public transport occupies a disproportionate amount of time.

There are, of course, many exceptions. Many people, especially in a creative business such as ours, put in long hours to get the job done.

But part of the problem I have with holidays is that I don't like them very much myself, unless I can also do some work. A couple of days on the beach and I'm desperate to get a pencil in my hand again.

To quote Alcibiades, 'In the service of Athens the few of quality who might have served well held back, abandoning the field to those whose greed for eminence was exceeded only by their lack of scruple in its pursuit.'
In the service of Terence, there were more than enough of the latter. Picking people is as much art as science. Who were his 'few of quality', how did he recognize them and how does he remember them?
GEOFF DAVY

Well, this is probably going to put a few noses out of joint.

Every entrepreneur knows that having the right team around them is fundamental to success. I have always looked for people who can work in a team and inspire others; people who are prepared to get their hands dirty and set an example; people who are unpretentious and honest; people who are creative, ambitious for the right reasons, and prepared to be involved in detail. People who are responsible and happy to admit it when they are wrong. People without chips on their shoulders; people with a sense of humour.

John Stephenson was terrific in the early days of the Design Group. John Mawer helped get Habitat on the rails, as did Maurice Libby and you, Geoff, who should have continued to run it rather than getting BhS'ed. Pauline Dora ran Conran's in America with devotion and Stafford Cliff and Oliver Gregory both did a remarkable job in the Design Group. Many architects and designers in our office today have terrific talent. I could fill a book with those who have made great contributions to the various businesses with which I have been involved over the last fifty years. I could fill another book with villains.

We have a fantastic team in our business at the moment, but I will only mention the chief executive, Des Gunewardena. If I had had him by my side since I began, I would have avoided a lot of the hiccups that have upset my career from time to time.

Having been a designer at the Conran Design Group, I couldn't help but be in awe of the many successful designers that have been through the Conran system. In the light of this, do you feel that you leave the design industry in safe hands?
JAMES PYOTT

Many designers and architects have worked at our desks since I first began what was then the Conran Design Group in 1956. David Chaloner, who also used to work with us, told me the other day that he had worked out that eight thousand designers have been employed by us over the last forty-five years, so I can well believe that a large number of design companies are now managed by ex-Conran designers. I am very proud to have seen the creative industries expand to such an extent in this country. As long as people like you are constantly striving to improve things, and never allow complacency to settle in, the industry is in very safe hands.

You are still controlling the interests of the Conran organizations and the avenues they pursue. Is there something that motivates you beyond the typical retirement age?
PAUL SIMMS

While I am executive chairman of Conran Holdings and, with my family, control ninety-two per cent of the shareholding, I am concerned about how the company will develop in the future. I hope I have planned for this wisely.

It's difficult to plan for your departure. Sometimes I think that a dramatic exit, where I clear my desk and sell all my shares, would be the best for everybody, including me. Then I realize that I love the business and many of the people in it and I'd feel lonely and bored without it.

People are fundamental to every business, but especially one that is so involved with creativity and service. I have tried to choose senior people that really understand the philosophy of the company and will continue to develop it, rather than let it stagnate, when I eventually go. One of the problems of being so identified with the business is that journalists always want to interview me rather than our chief executive, Des Gunewardena. I'm trying to overcome this; when he does become a media personality, at least he will have youth and good looks on his side, as well as a quick brain. He's also much more tactful than me, but perhaps that's a disadvantage where the media are concerned!

In the meantime, I am trying to withdraw very gradually, by attending fewer meetings and establishing a second office at my house in the country, where I can spend more time designing. One of the advantages of a slow withdrawal is that I can keep a beady eye on people and how things are progressing, while encouraging people to make decisions themselves. All businesses go through change, but it has to be slow and well managed. I've seen companies really suffer when new management arrives and changes everything dramatically, often with disastrous and even terminal results.

Being a private company with a family-controlled shareholding is an asset in this situation because change can be managed without the intense scrutiny of the press, analysts and institutional shareholders. We have a strong team, which is getting stronger all the time. Eventually I shall be able to slip away without anybody noticing or missing me. I do hope not!

Is the business more than just the man? Surely it would not be able to continue as it is without Conran the designer and entrepreneur at the helm?

RUPERT STEINER

Every entrepreneur likes to believe that their business will collapse without their hand on the tiller and I suppose that I am no exception! However, having come to the sad conclusion that I am not immortal, I have begun the process of encouraging other hands to steer the boat while I keep a close watch on the compass.

I believe the 'Conran' brand will survive as long as there are talented, entrepreneurial and ambitious people in the business, who see merit in the brand and the philosophy behind it and are excited by the challenge of developing it further.

When you were fifty you said you intended to retire at sixty. At seventy you have just set up and staffed a whole new office at your home. I don't believe you will ever retire, but perhaps you have plans to spend more time at leisure?

SEAN SUTCLIFFE

I hope I never retire in the conventional sense – I'd much rather die with an unfinished project on the drawing board. But I would like more time to visit museums and art galleries and to have long lunches with garrulous friends.

Which single piece of design would you like to be remembered for?
ANDREW SUMMERS

Difficult – probably a simple table called Bibliotheque, made by Benchmark.

In early childhood you threw stones at your sister's window at midnight so that she could assist you with the firing of your home-made kiln. Later came furniture design and production, Habitat, entrepreneurial retailing, shops and restaurants. Which part of this richly embroidered tapestry have you personally enjoyed the most?
PHILIP CUTLER

It's hard to choose from a lifetime of fun. When you commissioned me to design a collection of American-made products for Macy's, I remember being amazed to see it come together on the shop floor, after all the trials and tribulations we went through. Today, I get most satisfaction from Benchmark, our little furniture factory housed in the old agricultural buildings at my house in the country. It makes many of my designs and I really enjoy that hands-on approach, and working with people who make things and use their intelligence and experience to solve problems. Making things always seems more worthwhile than retailing them; combining the two is the best of both worlds.

What are your ambitions for the future?
JOHN SORRELL

Ten years of uninterrupted design work, mainly furniture and domestic products, and perhaps opening one last, very personal, restaurant.

My sketch for the Bibliotheque table, so called because the detailing of the legs reminds me of open books and thus the Parisian grand projet. Edward Gibbon, who wrote The Decline and Fall of the Roman Empire, was one of my ancestors.

SELF-PORTRAIT

André François, the well-known French cartoonist, puts me to bed in his slipper.

What follows is most definitely the 'warts and all' section of this book. In my replies to the personal questions asked by those nearest and dearest and those not so near and dear, I realize that I've exposed not only my warts, but my contradictions. I have often been told that I have a rather contradictory nature, and here is ample evidence of it.

Which ten words would come to mind if you were to describe yourself?
TOM FORD

Ambitious, mean, kind, greedy, frustrated, emotional, tiresome, intolerant, shy, fat.

Terence – you are often thought to be a bit arrogant, even rude. Is this a reflection of impatience with fools or with poor standards, or a fundamental shyness?
PRUE LEITH

Oh dear. I am quite shy and I don't really enjoy talking to people I don't know. A cocktail party with lots of people shouting banalities is my idea of hell. I would certainly try not to be rude to anybody unless they had been rude to me first – I hate rudeness as much as snobbery.

I hate to think that I can be perceived as arrogant – I despise this in others. But I have to agree that I do not suffer fools gladly, which may well be interpreted as arrogance. I don't think I could ever be *thoroughly* arrogant because I'm a war child and I remember the postwar years as a time when it was very difficult to achieve anything. Consequently, when I do get an opportunity, however small, I still remain surprised and grateful. I don't have a particularly high opinion of my talent, intelligence or achievements. I still try hard.

Do you have any dreams that you still wish to fulfil?
TOM CONRAN

I have never had a list of dreams or objectives and, even if I had, I couldn't cross any of them off as I am constantly dissatisfied with practically everything I do and continually try to do things better. I'm quite sure I will die dissatisfied!

Which one attribute of your personality would you say is the most important contributor to your success?
ELKIN PIANIM

A discerning and confident eye.

What is your most painful source of self-doubt?

MURIEL GRAY

My clarity of vision.

STAFFORD CLIFF:

What is your Achilles heel?

Impatience.

People say you're restless and unable to relax. Why is that and do you regret it?

There's just so much I want to do, things I want to see and books I want to read. I hate wasting time. On the other hand, I do like thinking in the sun, swimming and long meals with amusing friends. I also like playing chess.

Do you have a recurring nightmare, or an equivalent to the actor's dream of not knowing their lines or having a script?

I don't have recurring nightmares, but if I did they might well be about knowing my lines or reading from a script. I can't learn lines at all and I hate reading from a prepared text. On the other hand, I don't mind answering questions, which was one of the things that gave me the idea for this book.

As you like to remind those of us in your employ, you seldom stop working – weekends, holidays, all the time. Clearly you don't need to put yourself under that pressure any more, so what drives you to do this?

WENDY JONES

When you have suffered extreme frustration in your youth, you cannot believe that success, when it does eventually arrive, is anything permanent and so you keep grabbing your good luck while it is still around. There always seems to be something better and more exciting around the corner. The older you get, the more you realize the less you know, and this has the effect on me of making me want to do more.

I am lucky in that practically everything I do in my business life I would also do for pleasure: designing, writing, eating, drinking, shopping, travelling, gardening, even smoking cigars are all connected in some way to my work. I can't think of anything I would rather do. The secret is that I enjoy my work in the way other people enjoy their hobbies. I would much rather design things than play golf; I'd rather write books than watch football and I'd rather make furniture than ski. When you are doing things that interest you energy seems to come naturally.

I have always admired your will to succeed and to rebound from adversity. How far is this your nature, and how far a reaction to parents or environment? Has a (comparative) lack of academic success been a spur or a hindrance?

MICHAEL LIKIERMAN

Rather like you, I have had several setbacks in my life. On occasions I have thought about retiring from the fray and running a restaurant in the country, a small pottery or furniture workshop, or just being a designer, but then the lure of the marketplace resurges, aided by a determination to demonstrate that I wasn't wrong. This may well be arrogance on my part. My mother was always proud of my success and certainly, when she was alive, I was motivated by her pride.

Academic success is not necessarily an advantage in the world of business, chiefly because academics often take a theoretical approach to problem-solving rather than a practical one. People with highly intellectual backgrounds sometimes have difficulty understanding how those with non-academic backgrounds behave. Although exam results, upon which such stress is laid these days, demonstrate the ability of a student to learn, much of what is conventionally taught in schools has to be relearned in later life: it is the learning process itself that is of real and lasting value.

What keeps you so young?

LAURENCE ISAACSON

I am quite sure that having a life full of absorbing projects is the best way of feeling young. It keeps the adrenaline pumping and makes you want to jump out of bed in the morning.

Most of the people who work with me are in their twenties and thirties. On bad days this can have the effect of making you feel old and passé; on good days it can make you feel brighter and cleverer than they are! It also helps (most of the time) to be married to someone much younger and still to have teenage children about the house. Of course, sometimes this can also have the reverse effect and make me feel even older than I am.

Two of my eight grandchildren. Coco (LEFT), Sophie's daughter, dressed as a cat. Finbar (BELOW), Ned's eldest son, being inquisitive.

SOPHIE CONRAN:
What makes you happiest?

The vegetable garden coming to life in April after the long winter, the smell of freshly cut grass and blossom on the fruit trees.

Coco laughing.

Finally seeing something that I have designed in three dimensions.

A family lunch.

What makes you saddest?

The death of close friends, such as Michael Wickham and Oliver Gregory and especially my parents.

The abuse of the countryside, hideous housing developments.

What do you hate the most?
NED CONRAN

Bureaucracy, dishonesty, pretentiousness, disinterest.

What do you dislike most about the modern world?
TOM FORD

The huge divergence in living standards between rich and poor nations.

The conservatory at Shad Thames is a particularly peaceful place, good for quiet contemplation and cigar smoking.

THE OATES FAMILY:
What do you do to cheer yourself up?

Sit in the greenhouse and smoke a cigar and read a good book. Maybe have a glass of vieille prune as well, then design a bit of furniture.

What has been your most embarrassing moment?

Discovering that I had grown out of feeling embarrassed.

Do you ever talk to Spot when no one else is around?

Yes. (Spot is the terrier who belongs to my stepdaughter, Hattie.)

You obviously enjoy many of the good things in life – good food and drink, beautiful women, fast cars, beautiful design, a good cigar. You give the impression of being able to get pleasure out of a huge range of life's activities, but you can't enjoy everything: what is it in life that really frightens you? It's often said that highly creative people use their gift to exorcize some kind of personal demon. Do you think that's true, and if it is, what are your personal demons?

ROGER MAVITY

'Frighten' is perhaps too strong a word, but I dislike it when things are out of control, whether in my personal life or business life, or outside my life altogether. That sense of being out of control probably accounts for the fact that I found being driven rather fast in a car on Indian roads at night a pretty terrifying experience.

I'm not aware of exorcizing any demons, but a large part of what motivates me is frustration. Frustration that I have many ideas but not enough time to carry them through.

Apart from rugby union, what do you enjoy watching on television? What kind of music do you like to listen to?

DIANE AND IAN SMITH

I like to watch the History and Discovery channels, the news, good films and drama series such as *Love in a Cold Climate*, *Inspector Morse* and *Frost*. I hate game shows and soaps. My favourite type of music is jazz; Vicki likes seventeenth- and eighteenth-century music, which I enjoy too, most of the time.

If you were to appear on *Stars In Their Eyes*, who would you be and what would you sing?

STEVEN BLACKMAN

I think I'd like to be Hutch in the old Quaglino's in the 1930s. I'd sing 'Smoke Gets In Your Eyes' to all the young debs, who would listen with pent-up pleasure and desire.

MAGGIE HEANEY:

Have you ever found being such an arbiter of taste and style a burden? Do you ever crave baked beans on toast, TV and rather questionable slippers?

As far as taste is concerned, I can only show people what I like and I don't find this a burden at all. I can't tell people what they *should* like, that's for them to decide. I certainly live a fairly simple life at home. Eating supper in front of the telly with my slippers on is a great pleasure, but I do prefer cassoulet to baked beans.

Although one loved you to bits, at times you could be quite terrifying to work for. I still have that rather frightening photograph of you in my loo; it has long been my laxative! What or who has the same effect on you?

Jerusalem artichokes and reheated Indian food.

You have a very dry wit; who or what makes you laugh?

Crude, racy jokes told by the Irish. Paul Merton.

Once, in Paris, you showed me some carvings in an antique shop that you said you coveted more than anything, yet you did not buy them. Do you covet things today and still walk away? In a lifetime so dedicated to design, where even a simple and functional item was chosen with such care and passion, which one possession would you hate to part with above all others?

I'm certainly going through a stage in my life when I'm de-accessioning, as the museums put it. I have always had a passion for *objets trouvés*, but life can get silted up with them. I've recently had a great clearout at my house in the country and the effect has been exhilarating. Although I have many treasured possessions, by and large I have few really valuable things, as these only make life more complicated. I guess that's the reason I didn't buy the carvings.

At the moment my favourite possessions are nineteen Bugatti pedal cars that are hung in the entrance hall of my house in the country. They have wonderful shapes and many work in different ways; I always smile when I see them lined up rather like a collection of beautiful hawk moths. The French collector from whom I bought them took quite some persuading that I would give them a good home and the love, attention and dusting they deserve. I have dreams of a great pedal car race, with nineteen children pedalling

Currently among my most treasured possessions are these Bugatti pedal cars, which I acquired from a French collector and nineteen of which now hang on the wall in the entrance hall at Barton Court. They somehow remind me of beautiful moths.

furiously down dusty lanes, the winner commemorated in a ceramic plaque in the Michelin Building.

I am sitting here surrounded by beautiful things with sentimental associations: a knife from Jasper, a game of carpet croquet from Sebastian, a pestle and mortar from Tom, a lacquer box from Sophie, a picture painted by Ned, a glass bowl from Vicki. Where would I begin to choose? If I were being completely unsentimental about it, I would probably pick the Karuselli chair that I sit in every night. I'd be lost without it.

What are the five most important things you use everyday?
ILSE CRAWFORD

Shoes, trousers, shirt, light, pen. I can't stop at five. Chair, car, cup, cooking pan, glass, knife, cigar, bath, bed.

It's 2031. Medical students are making skipping ropes from your intestines, your skeleton is being prodded by anatomists, but your soul flies up to Heaven and it turns out that there is a God. How would you want Him to judge you? And – having secured your place in Heaven – what will the obituarists have written that makes you most proud?
SIMON WILLIS

I would certainly be astonished to find that there is a God. I believe man created God, not the other way round, and that organized religion has been the cause of many of the world's problems, historically and currently. So before God judged me, I would like to ask Him a few questions first. I would certainly like to know if He considers Himself omnipotent, with the power to control people's destinies. And, if so, then why does He do such a lousy job and allow so much evil, misery and poverty to exist in what is supposed to be His kingdom? If I got a satisfactory answer to that one, I'd be happy to be judged and consigned straight to Hell!

I'd be very proud to read over the shoulder of my obituarists that I had been a good, practical designer of useful things. And, P S, thanks for another thirty years!

TOM CONRAN:

I know that essentially you are an atheist, but do you have any beliefs regarding the spiritual side of life?

I don't think I have ever had any truly spiritual experience myself, except for those odd coincidences such as *déjà vu*, or suddenly thinking about someone out of the blue and running into them the day after.

Ultimately I believe that everything has a scientific explanation, although science does not entirely account for our moral sense and our distinction between right and wrong. Whether we will ever unravel all the secrets of the universe, I just do not know. But in many ways, it is good to have mystery in our lives; it stops us from becoming complacent.

What is your ideal form of government?

I think that our present democratic system in Britain is more or less right. What I do worry about is whether it can ever be truly effective with the constant barrage of aggressive media scrutiny. Who in their right mind would want to be a politician at the moment? And, given this situation, how will we ever get the best people to come forward to run the country?

By strange coincidence, a three-party tie has been the result of a general election. No amount of recounts will deliver an outright winner. You have an opportunity to choose a cabinet. Who will get which post and why?

VICKI CONRAN

I am glad to say that this will never happen. At any rate, I do not believe a coalition government can work in peacetime. Just as in business, you need a strong leader with a philosophy, and he or she has to choose a group of people to work with who share this philosophy, and who can develop and enforce it. While I could put together a list of the great and the good, I know quite well that many would not want to waste their time in a political wasps' nest, with very little chance of being able to achieve anything worthwhile. Running a country is probably the most complex management task there is, but the principles are the same as running a business or a football team, neither of which could survive or succeed with the structure you propose.

Is it true you were offered a knighthood during the Falklands War by Margaret Thatcher's government and turned it down? If so, was this on moral grounds or political, and would your decision have been different had a Labour government been in power?

JONATHAN CHIDSEY

I wasn't offered a knighthood, I was asked to *lunch* at Downing Street by Margaret Thatcher. It was during the Falklands War and I turned the invitation down on moral grounds. Had a Labour government been in power, I would also have turned down the invitation; but if they had, I hope they would have resolved the dispute diplomatically without having to resort to force.

Your empire has been built in urban environments, employing many young people over the years. Do you think that business has a responsibility to assist in the rejuvenation of city centres or to help deal with issues such as homelessness? Do you get involved and if so, in what way?

WENDY HOWLAND JACKSON

I hope that anyone who lives or trades in a city would take an interest in its rejuvenation. I certainly do. In many cases, simply the presence of a business in a run-down or neglected part of the city can help to effect a transformation. Our development at Butlers Wharf was a case in point.

As far as the problem of homelessness is concerned, we have donated money and food and once lent a building to be used as a shelter over Christmas, but these efforts are mere drops in a disgracefully empty bucket. Apart from transport, homelessness is London's greatest problem and despite the city's affluence, I see no real sign that it is being resolved. On the personal side, I feel the best I can do is to raise the issue with influential people I meet; I also discussed the subject in some detail in my book on London. At least our newish Mayor understands and seems determined to find and implement a solution.

As the man responsible for introducing style into both British homes and restaurants, do you think style is more important than substance in politics?

MO MOWLAM

Style without substance is worthless. Substance without style can be pretty boring. Is this a loaded question?

You've been very influenced by European styles in food and design. Do you think that our legal system (which is totally different from the Napoleonic Code that holds sway in most European countries) should become more European?

MICHAEL HAYES

I have very little knowledge of the complexities of European law, although through trading and living in different European countries I have discovered just how different they are. If we want to create a proper European union and free trade area, and I hope that we do, then it would seem to me that the single most important requirement would be to have a unification of laws throughout member states.

Change might need to happen on both sides. For instance, there are certain aspects of the Napoleonic Code that may have been appropriate in Napoleon's day, but seem less so today. In particular, I'm thinking of the laws regarding the inheritance of property and the damage they have done to French agriculture and rural communities.

You must be used to compliments, but what's the best-ever compliment you've received?

MOONEY

The best was definitely being made a Commander of Arts and Letters by the French Minister of Culture, Jack Lang. Recognition by a foreign government came as a great surprise. The charming ceremony at the French embassy, organized by the ambassador and to which my family and friends were invited, meant so much more to me than being part of a production line in a hideous room in Buckingham Palace and waiting to be tapped on the shoulder by our Queen.

You are an outstandingly wealthy man. Is there any guilt associated with the personal retention of such wealth?

MURIEL GRAY

I don't feel guilty about it at all, but I never really think about it in terms of personal money or personal wealth. Most of it is paper money, at any rate, in the form of shares that could become worthless overnight. When Habitat was floated on the Stock Exchange and I made some serious money, I donated £20 million to set up the Conran Foundation and Design Museum; I've got some other reasonably altruistic things planned.

A few of my favourite things: the simple joys of bluebell woods and log fires.

I just wonder what you have enjoyed doing the most? You can't have done it all just to make money?

JEAN BARROW

I've never done anything solely for the purpose of making money; survival yes, getting rich no. When I have compromised in my work for financial reasons, things have usually not gone well and I have been disappointed in the result and in myself. I was obviously not born to be a capitalist, although I recognized fairly early on in my career that if you didn't make a profit, you were unlikely to survive in business. Essentially, I like making money so that I can spend it on more projects. I am really not very good at spending money on myself.

What I have enjoyed most are those projects where I have been able to be involved in every tiny detail. That kind of commitment and passion keeps me going.

You enjoy many of the privileges that wealth and success bring. Do you think you are in touch with 'ordinary life'? Can you give me some examples?

SIMON WILLIS

I don't know how you define 'ordinary'. I've never met an ordinary person yet; have you? I think that when you work in a business that employs thousands of people and has millions of customers it's practically impossible to be isolated from real life, even if you wanted to be, which I certainly don't. My working life brings me in contact with lots of different sorts of people from all sorts of backgrounds and with all sorts of different skills. And, like most people, I try and keep myself as informed as possible by reading a lot of newspapers and magazines, listening to the news and looking at research on social trends.

Do you believe in the 'simple pleasures' of life? And, if so, what are they?

GEORGIA GLYNN SMITH

Meadows and sunshine, bubbling streams, sandy beaches, bluebell woods, torrential rain, snow-covered hills, bread and cheese, being a *flâneur* in a foreign town, sleeping in fresh white linen sheets, sitting in front of a log fire . . . In fact, I like the simple pleasures so much I wrote a book about them called *Easy Living*.

Are you happy to be called a hedonist?

GHISLAINE BAVOILLOT

I think it is probably a very fair description. I'm a hard-working hedonist, if that isn't an oxymoron, and one whose tastes are hedonistically monastic, if that isn't another.

In which period of your life were you happiest about your appearance?

ALICE RAWSTHORN

I really have never been much interested in my appearance, but in the mid-1950s I was influenced by a rather dapper chap called Brinsley Black, a deb's delight who was the sales manager of my first showroom in the Piccadilly Arcade. We had suits made to my design at the fifty-shilling tailor's and both appeared in *Tailor and Cutter*.

Why do you always wear blue shirts?

MARK BOND

For aesthetic and practical reasons: I like the colour and they don't show the dirt.

How many blue shirts do you own?

VITTORIO RADICE

At the last count, forty-two. I never throw any away, as I particularly like them when they are frayed around the collar and cuffs!

I would like to ask you about your neckties. It is well known that one of your mannerisms is, or for years and years was, only to wear ties with spots (the spots being part of their design, that is, not accidental droppings). I can see the advantage of this for a busy man; it saves having to choose which pattern to wear round your neck when getting dressed. But I'd like to know (a) when this habit began and (b) how, as a design-conscious and fairly fashion-conscious man, you can bear to be stuck with the same old spotted ties, day in and out, even if the colours are different.

Ever since my earliest days as a designer, when I was trying to persuade bank managers to take me seriously, I've never been a particularly flamboyant dresser: hence my loyalty to blue shirts and spotted ties.

Have you never broken this rule? Will you ever? Or maybe you *have* changed your spots since the last time I saw you.

SUSAN CAMPBELL

I've never been a very racy dresser. This is partly because from an early age I wanted to be taken seriously as a designer and felt that dressing in a rather flamboyant and bohemian way would not further my cause.

Someone gave me a silk spotted tie from Turnbull & Asser in the early 1970s and the first time I wore it, I thought, 'this is my sort of tie'; over the years, I've acquired about fifty in various colours. They are quite good at camouflaging the spots of food that seem magnetically attracted to them. I do rather admire the Jon Snows of this world who look like walking art galleries – and I did change a spot for a small oval the other day. But I actually prefer wearing open-necked shirts and would rather not wear a tie at all if I can get away with it.

You once said in a newspaper that one of the things you most wanted for Christmas was a pair of Nike trainers. You are not known for your jogging, so does this mean that trainers are your chosen weekend footwear for going shopping in Kintbury?
DES GUNEWARDENA

What I actually *said* was that I would like a pair of very plain gym shoes, with plain blue canvas uppers and plain white rubber soles. This got illustrated with a picture of a nice pair of Nike trainers that were a bit smarter than the shoes I had in mind and made me feel like I should be taking up jogging. I usually wear very worn-out brown loafers with holes in the soles. I did once design some rather smart shoes for Tim Little called 'Kangaroo', made of kangaroo hide, and these do bring a spring to my step.

When, why and what started you on the cigars we see you enjoying in photographs?
PETER ROWAN

I think somebody gave me a cigar on the opening night of Habitat in 1964. I liked it and gradually smoked more. I'm afraid I came to the expensive conclusion that Havanas were the best. I like to think that, because I don't inhale, they don't do me much harm. They give me much the same soothing and pleasing sensation as the smell of a winter bonfire of fallen leaves gives most people.

I have smoked Havana cigars for about the last forty years and they have become as integral to my life as a cup of coffee or a glass of wine. I *can* live without them and on several occasions I have not smoked a cigar for a week or so, not by my own choice, but due to circumstances beyond my control. However, I feel that life with Hoyo de Monterrey, Epicure No. 2 is just more pleasant in every way.

Havana cigars are one product category that has escaped the attentions of designers, in some cases for nearly a century. Do you think this has done them any harm?
SIMON CHASE

There are many books that celebrate the wonderful Victorian graphics of cigar labels and packaging. The intricate and rather naive charm of these designs lends a welcome counterpoint to the product, just as a Patrick Caulfield painting might provide for a modernist interior. But, as the relatively recent design for the Cohiba cigar label and packaging demonstrates, contemporary design can also be appropriate: I love it, and the content, too. I was especially pleased to see it written about the other day as the 'Habitat' cigar.

Comp Lit Habana.

SIR LES PATTERSON:

Come clean, Terry, as a bloke who makes beds, have you found your fame has got you a lot more mattress action than you would've otherwise enjoyed?

As you will know, Les, a knighthood, fame and fortune are even more potent than oysters, even those Aussie ones that fill your mouth and throat.

Have you ever done the dirty deed in one of your outlets after trading hours with a trusted Girl Friday?

Yes.

I love your nosh-houses, especially Guastavino's in New York, which I have visited many times with assorted research assistants thanks to the munificence of the Australian taxpayer. Do you choose the menus yourself and, if so, what is it you slip in the soup? I've got lucky after every meal, and I mean lucky!

I choose the menus with the help of my lascivious chefs. I always find a little chilli stimulates the appetite.

Simone Signoret.

Who is the most beautiful woman you have ever met?
SEBASTIAN CONRAN

Simone Signoret, who looked rather like your mother before she became a Superwoman.

Women or cigars?
SIMON WILLIS

Rudyard Kipling may have said, 'A woman is only a woman, but a good cigar is a smoke', but I've never found them to be mutually exclusive. I think they go together very well.

MURIEL GRAY:
There's a perception of you that you are passionate about design and objects, and less so about people and emotions. Is this unfair?

Products *should* be designed by people with passion. I keep my own emotions fairly under control, but they seethe inside, I promise you!

Are you, or were you, a sexual man, or simply sensual?

Don't they go hand in hand? I hope I've still got a bit of both sides to me – but for how much longer?

Were you a good father?

By today's standards, probably not. By the standards of thirty to forty years ago, reasonably good. I like to think that I've always had a good relationship with all my children – certainly my children say that I have been a good father to them and who am I to argue? – but they also say that they missed me when they were growing up because I was often away and busy. I was having a conversation with my son Tom about this quite recently, as he himself was about to become a father. He said that he always felt that I was not at home enough when he was young.

I think I always felt pulled in two directions. If your work involves taking risks, like mine, it's difficult to set aside enough time for family life; if you've got a job with a fixed income

LEFT TO RIGHT: *Tom, Caroline, me, Kasmin's son Paul and Mrs Stephen Buckley.*

and fixed parameters, on the other hand, then it's much easier to tailor your life to fit and accommodate that side of things. When most of my children were young, I was constantly worried either about money or the future of the business, which made it difficult to take time off. Probably the worst to suffer in this respect were my two eldest children, Sebastian and Jasper, who did get bounced around like shuttlecocks between Shirley and myself once her interest in journalism began to take over. Caroline, however, who was altogether more of a maternal person, gave up her job at Habitat when Tom was born and provided a very stable background for the whole family.

Now we still have Vicki's three children living at home; I see Sebastian every day in the office and the others on a fairly regular basis. Jasper tends to be around a lot, or not at all. Shirley has remarked that people are better at being parents at different ages, and perhaps this is true.

I suppose I would define a good father as someone who loves and inspires his children. I certainly love my children, and my grandchildren, although you would have to ask them whether or not I have been a source of inspiration.

Caroline and me with all the children. LEFT TO RIGHT: *Ned, Sophie, Jasper, Sebastian and Tom.*

Did your son's homosexuality cause you any distress?

Not in the least. I have had many gay friends and it didn't come as any sort of surprise to me. In fact, I find it quite natural and about as relevant as him being, say, left-handed.

Terry dearest, your son Jasper has gone into the same profession, *haute couture*, as my darling son Kenny. We are both proud and supportive parents but we've had to make emotional and philosophical adjustments in accepting our gifted bachelor boys and their flatmates. With our natural desire to become caring grandparents, what can we do to hurry our hesitant sons into matrimony?

DAME EDNA EVERAGE

My son Jasper tried matrimony once. It didn't entirely agree with him, but it did produce a lovely little green card that he cherished. I'm glad, however, to have him back in the nest, as he is just as loveable as any little grandchild.

In any event, I am already a grandfather, several times over. My son Sebastian has two children, Sam and Max; then there's Sophie's two, Felix and Coco; Ned's sons Finbar and Harry and daughter Rose, and Tom's new baby daughter, Iris May.

What does 'family' mean to you?
DAPHNE OATES

Firstly, Vicki and our children; secondly, those people I work with closely, who also become a sort of family too.

Having been married more than once, how have you found dealing with stepchildren?
MO MOWLAM

I have only inherited one set of stepchildren, Vicki's, and found them totally charming, even when going through that particularly difficult teenage period. But I know I'm lucky and this is certainly not always the case. Both Caroline and Vicki have been particularly excellent stepmothers to my children from previous marriages, despite the difficulties these inherited families often cause.

I know the children feel particularly fond of their stepmothers and they are all happy to benefit considerably at birthdays, Christmases and so on. More in this case is definitely better!

You appear to have a very strong bond with your children, both in a positive and negative sense. Is it true that you are still competing with each other in the Conran clan?
COLIN TWEEDY

All my children have been given shares in the business and take an interest in its progress and success. Sebastian, my eldest son, is a director of Conran & Partners, our design and architectural company, and most of the others, including Jasper, have been involved in projects connected with the company over the years.

They are all talented people in their own right and many of them have set up companies in areas that are similar to the fields in which I operate, but that are not directly competitive. We all seem to share many of the same ideas and ambitions; even my sister,

With Jasper, Tom, Sophie and Sebastian at our apartment in London.

with her Carluccio's Caffès, ploughs a parallel furrow. Although I have never deliberately tried to encourage my children to take up professional interests similar to my own, they seem to have absorbed it by osmosis. Sometimes I wish one of them had become an accountant or a lawyer!

I'm not aware of there being a negative side to the bond between us. From the outside, it may appear that we compete with each other and there probably is a bit of amicable sibling rivalry that goes on, but generally we all get on very well together and love and support each other.

What is the most satisfying present you have ever given?
GEORGIA GLYNN SMITH

I gave my son Tom a house we'd owned in the Dordogne. I loved the house and so does he. I know he gets a lot of pleasure from it, which of course gives pleasure to me.

Vicki and I laughing at the paparazzi.

If you could ask somebody only one question, what would it be?
HATTIE GALLAGHER

'Do you love me?'

What quality in your friends do you most admire?
PAULA PRYKE

Their *joie de vivre*.

Who is your closest friend?
MURIEL GRAY

My wife, because we can and do discuss anything and everything.

Would you ever consider remarriage?

PAUL SIMMS

I have 'remarried' quite a number of times. I'm currently married to Vicki and hope to be for the rest of my life. I've never broken off a marriage, which probably indicates that I'm pretty difficult to live with!

Your question may reflect the notoriety that surrounded my last divorce. Divorce, I imagine, is practically always upsetting, and my last divorce was certainly very upsetting indeed. My wife Caroline and I had been married for thirty years and had three children. Although we lived fairly separate lives, she with her beautiful house in Dorset, me most of the time working in London, we met at Barton Court at the weekends and got on, I thought, pretty well. Then on our thirtieth anniversary, she upped and left. No word of explanation, and there never has been.

Although I was devastated, we remained on good terms. We both wanted an amicable divorce and settlement and did not want to go to court. Then the lawyers got involved. My lawyer eventually received a list of demands from her lawyer that were so extravagant that court was the only solution.

When it came to court, her lawyer played the 'contribution' card to the hilt; great play was made of the fact that Caroline had cooked a few meals for the Habitat buyers. Although I was happy to agree that in the very early, pre-opening days of Habitat, Caroline had had an involvement in the business, over the years she had increasingly shown a marked antipathy to any commercial enterprise and certainly ones that I was involved in. While I believe that every divorcée should get proper financial support from their partner that should allow them, if possible, to live as they did before, the whole issue of 'contribution' needs to be dealt with sensitively or it can ruin the business and life of at least one of the partners. In my case, the judge paid no regard to the fact that I had given my wife twenty-four per cent of my company on our marriage, refused leave to appeal and published his judgement immediately rather than waiting the normal six months so that it would generate maximum publicity. It did.

After the divorce, I made a great mistake in complaining about the judgement publicly, querying the issue of contribution by saying that it amounted to Caroline cooking a few meals for Habitat buyers. The press gleefully seized on this, but in their reports 'cooking a few meals for Habitat buyers' became 'cooking a few meals' full stop! I'm happy to put the record straight and state that she cooked many delicious meals for me and our children and friends.

My advice is don't get divorced, stay happily married. I intend to in the future.

Now you are the first British furniture megastar since Chippendale, have you discovered a downside to celebrity as I have. Forfeiture of privacy? Parasitical relationships (like mine with my bridesmaid Madge Allsop)? Sycophantic but untrustworthy advisers (like my manager Barry Humphries)? Are you able to delegate or do you really have to keep a personal eye on every transaction, however small?

DAME EDNA EVERAGE

As you say, dearest Edna, stardom does have its downside. Relationships certainly become more complex. Delegation is always the problem: too much and you get no satisfaction; too little and you get worn to a frazzle. The answer is to have a team around you who know you well enough to interpret your ideas without usurping your position, don't you find?

On the whole, I prefer privacy to any kind of fame. But from time to time notoriety allows you to meet interesting people and see interesting things. It sometimes gets you through airports quickly. (Question: Why am I doing this book?)

Town or country, and why?

MATTHEW WOOD

Both, if possible: the country allows you to recharge your batteries for city life. Town for energy, creativity, diversity, competitiveness, ambition, sociability, hard work and fun. Country for contemplation, communion, relaxation, quietness, comfort and joy. I do, though, regret the gulf that seems to have widened between town and country over issues such as hunting. Personally, I find the sight of huntsmen togged up to the nines blowing their horns hilarious – where would tablemat manufacturers be without them? But I believe the best way to deal with the 'sport' is to ridicule it out of existence.

I've lived in London almost all my adult life. Today I literally live 'over the shop', at the top of our building at Shad Thames, designed by Michael Hopkins and built by David Mellor. My apartment comprises the top two floors and has terraces that look out over St Saviour's Dock and the Thames; our design offices and contracts showroom are located on the first six floors; and Restaurant and Conran Shop offices, the Design Museum and Butlers Wharf gastrodrome are right round the corner.

Although my working life has largely been centred on the town, I've nearly always managed to maintain a place in the country. For a while I had a cottage in Dalham, Norfolk, near my furniture factory; later I had a farmhouse in France by the Dordogne river.

But I suppose I consider my true home to be Barton Court, in Kintbury near Hungerford. A large Georgian house, previously used as a boys' school, when I bought it in 1972 it was in a very poor state of repair. The roof had fallen in, the windows were broken and the whole place was redolent of dry rot and smacked bottoms. Because it was in such a dreadful condition, a major rebuilding project had to be undertaken.

One of the projects I have enjoyed most in recent years has been the conversion of the derelict farm buildings attached to Barton Court into workshops for Benchmark, our woodworking business. Many farm buildings across Britain lie unused and until recently planners have been cautious about giving permission for uses other than agricultural purposes. Benchmark has demonstrated how such redundant buildings can be successfully reused, both in terms of generating employment and in making economical use of old structures. Most importantly, for me at least, it means that I can make productive use of my time in the country and do what I enjoy the most, which is working.

Which room in your house is your favourite?

NORMAN FOSTER

I have a large room in the country that I use as an office with lots of books, a huge desk, a comfortable sofa, an open wood fire and views over the fields and the river.

Among your other achievements, you managed to find time to restore a farmhouse in Provence, creating an environment in which to relax, surrounded by colour and with the soothing trickle of water. What gave you the inspiration and what do you like about being at 'Brunelys'?

BOB WIGLEY

I found Brunelys in a rather roundabout way. Francis Bacon had been staying with us and one evening, while discussing our favourite houses, Francis waxed lyrical about a house he had stayed at near Salon in Provence, which belonged to another painter called Rodrigo Moynihan, whom I knew slightly through the Royal College.

Soon after, when I heard that Rodrigo wanted to sell this house, I got myself invited to see it. It was indeed a beautiful house with its own mulberry farm, but after we had stayed there a couple of days, I realized that with a huge number of hectares of land, large cherry orchards and about thirty employees, it was really a business rather than a holiday house.

With a certain degree of regret, Caroline and I retired to a local hotel to continue to enjoy the beautiful countryside. While we were having dinner on the terrace, a photographer I knew stopped at our table and asked us and some friends for a drink. I was then introduced to some people who ran Soleido, the well-known Provençal textile company in Tarascon. They wanted to know what we were doing in Provence and I told

Space, light and air in our apartment above the office in Butlers Wharf.

Part of the walled vegetable garden at Barton Court.

The garden (LEFT) and kitchen (BELOW) at Brunelys, our house in Provence.

them the story of the Moynihan house. They replied that they knew the most beautiful house in Provence and that coincidentally it was for sale. We arranged to meet the next day at the Bistro de Paradou for lunch and we were then taken to Brunelys, which was about a kilometre away.

The building was very basic, and consisted of two large barns connected by the farmer's living quarters. It was also in a derelict state – the walls seemed to be built of stone blotting paper and there were no amenities – so I could do what I wanted with it. But the really wonderful thing about the house was the land that surrounded it, about eighty hectares of hayfields bisected with little streams fed by the Canal de Provence and bounded by rows and rows of cypress trees. There were also about eight hundred olive trees and a long avenue of chestnuts; on either side the property was bordered by one of the last remaining Mediterranean forests and rocky hills covered with wild thyme and rosemary. The final bonus was the views of Les Alpilles, the extraordinary little mountains that look as though they were carved by Henry Moore. There were no other houses in sight.

I converted Brunelys very simply. One of the barns became a large living room and the other a huge kitchen. Behind the house I built a terraced garden with running water and a pool. I was particularly pleased that when the huge amount of building work was over and I gave a party for the locals, they seemed surprised and rather disappointed that they couldn't see any difference to what had been there before.

I love being at Brunelys; it's so relaxing and it has made such a wonderful place for the children's holidays over the last fifteen years. But I spend far too little time there. Because I have a wonderful house and garden in England, which is always at its best when we go to France, I am increasingly aware that having two houses (and a flat) is more than enough.

What is your worst memory of travelling? And your best?

ALICE RAWSTHORN

My worst journey was in the early 1960s. I was returning from Italy (a buying trip or a visit to Milan, I can't remember which) when the engine of my Alfa Romeo seized up on an obscure pass in the French Alps. It was the middle of the night and there was a snowstorm. I had raging toothache, no gloves or overcoat and there was nobody to be seen anywhere. I thought I was going to die.

I was so cold I dragged all my clothes out of my suitcase and put as many of them on as I could – layers of shirts, three pairs of underpants – and then I sat out the freezing night until eventually someone came by on the road and rescued me. As soon as I reached the nearest town and had arranged for a garage to retrieve the car, I went into a café. I have a vivid memory of eating pea and ham soup and drinking a large glass of brandy. My toothache vanished instantly.

My best travel experience was undoubtedly flying to Rio on French Concorde, with its elegant Raymond Loewy interior. The staff were all ex-Chanel models or Gregory Peck lookalikes and the food was simple and delicious.

Which cars have you most enjoyed, either driving yourself or being driven? Which do you prefer, driving yourself or from the back seat?
REG DIXSON

I have always enjoyed driving my 911 Porsche myself. I think the old BMW was probably the best car to be driven in by you, especially when you are being entrepreneurial, in other words when you forget to be the incredibly polite driver you are most of the time and indulge in a little creative cutting up! Our new Audi is shaping up well and I think it's got that extra bit of edge to save us from being late too often. I very much enjoy driving you from the back seat in London and driving myself in the country.

MAUREEN DOHERTY:
If you had been born a woman, which woman of the twentieth century would you choose to be?

Vita Sackville-West. Why? She had a remarkable style and eye that she used in many ways, particularly as a brilliant garden designer; she seemed to manage to negotiate her way through a fairly complex family and social life, and she wrote beautifully. If I had been her, how much more interesting my answers would have been.

Please describe your perfect morning. Where are you? How do you bathe? What do you eat?

Mornings are not often perfect. On the rare good ones, I wake up at about seven o'clock in my large bed, with clean white linen sheets, having slept well. Late spring sunshine comes through the windows and the room smells of the wisteria that covers the front of my house in the country. I look out and see that it's a fine, cloudless day and that there are swans and ducks on the river and somebody fishing on the bank.

I clean my teeth rather energetically. I put on my large white Indian cotton dressing gown and I go to the kitchen. I drink a large glass of freshly squeezed orange juice, eat a bowl of muesli and drink several cups of tea. I read a couple of newspapers.

Looking for God? A photograph of the sky over our house in Provence taken by my stepson Toby Gallagher.

I then have a bath in a very large tub, filled to the top with quite hot water, shave and wash my hair with something that smells good, dry myself with a large white fluffy towel and put on some large, well-used clothes. I then brush what's left of my hair with a nice wooden-backed brush and slap some Acqua di Parma on my cheeks if I remember.

What would be your perfect day?

MICHAEL BLOOMBERG

It would be springtime. I'd spend the morning driving around Burgundy in an open-top car, visiting a few vineyards and tasting a few wines. Lunch would be a picnic by the canal in a cowslip meadow, followed by a sleep in the grass after drinking too much wine. I might draw a bit of nature in rather a frivolous way with a 2B pencil. Then I'd find a nice simple hotel with big airy rooms and views over the countryside where I could have a wonderful Burgundian meal, lasting at least three hours. I'd drink lots of old Burgundy and a bit of marc, and finally fall into a huge bed with crisp white sheets with the one I love to sleep the night through without a care in the world.

What would be the menu for your perfect meal? Where would you eat it? And with whom would you be sharing it?

ROGER MAVITY

A shaded table, a sunny view in early autumn, a smouldering log fire. Plain white, well-starched tablecloth and napkins, thin white plates and silver cutlery, very sharp, carbon steel knife blades. A large plate of Scottish langoustines. A salad made with huge Provençal tomatoes, my own olive oil and a squeeze of lemon, plenty of sea salt. A roast grouse with proper bread sauce, gravy and game chips and a big bunch of glossy watercress. A perfect Camembert. A bowl of yellow autumn raspberries, a bottle of Batard-Montrachet and another of Romanée-Conti. An espresso or two, an Epicure No. 2, a vieille prune and off to bed. I am always happy to eat with Vicki but I quite like eating by myself as it leaves plenty of room for thinking!

Where and with whom do you feel most happy?

NORMAN FOSTER

I feel pretty happy on the second day (the first is always filled with problems) in our house in France, when tensions seem to ooze away and I can lie by the warm pool in the early summer sunshine, drinking wine, reading a book and smoking a cigar. When you and Elena come to dinner with Vicki and me at Butlers Wharf, I'm even happier.

If you were stranded on a desert island, which is the one practical item you would like to have with you?

NICK ROBINSON

A very sharp knife. Then I could sharpen a stick so that I could design things in the wet sand and then begin all over again when the tide went out. I hope it would be an island near Cuba so that I could make my own cigars from wild tobacco leaves.

If you came back to earth, reincarnated, fifty years from now, on the condition that you could not be British or involve yourself in anything you had touched in your previous life, which nationality would you select and why? What one profession would you choose to excel in second time round?

NIGEL FRENCH

I think I would like to be Italian for the simple reason that I like the food, language and country. I would like to be a small farmer, producing olives, grapes, *porcini* and perhaps some *tartufi bianchi*. I'd also be a sculptor on the side.

Do you think you could have been happy if you hadn't been successful?

NED CONRAN

Yes. I could have been happy in a rural retreat, making pots and furniture and maybe cooking in a small restaurant. I can't prove it, of course, but I believe that I could.

I think of you as a designer – but you have also played out many other roles. If you had another life what would you explore as another profession?

NORMAN FOSTER

I don't expect another life, I am sad to say, but if I did, I would like to find a way of being a farmer; livestock, market gardening and architectural landscaping combined. Can I have a farm shop and restaurant, too? Perhaps I could come back as the Duchess of Devonshire!

My other project might be to gather together a group of like-minded, design-driven manufacturers of wood and metal products, printers, weavers, upholsterers, potters, glass and leather workers, plastics moulders, makers of electronic products, and build an excellent industrial complex where each company could benefit from the adjacency of the other. There would be a showroom-cum-retail space to generate revenue and part of the project would become an inspirational training centre and design studios. It would be an entirely modern equivalent of the William Morris vision. It would also learn from the Florentine pattern of many entrepreneurial small workshops dependent on each other's skills. It would encourage and renew excitement and passion for manufacture and become something of a focus for how New Labour could work in a new way.

If you were given two weeks to live, what would you do?

NED CONRAN

First of all I'd put my affairs in order. Then I'd see as many of my family and friends as possible and ask them to join me eating good food and drinking the best bottles in my cellar. I'd design my last piece of furniture. And I'd arrange a huge firework display for my last night.

Do you have any regrets?

JEFF HEADING

In my personal life I regret several broken marriages and the upset they have caused my children. Professionally: the loss of my furniture factory in Thetford and, later, the loss of Habitat; failing to turn BhS into a European Gap or to realize the full potential of Butlers Wharf.

If you had to do it all over again, would you?

TOM FORD

Yes, but with a large dose of hindsight.

You have lived the allotted three score and ten during a historic and dynamic period. Would you like to change those seventy years for another segment of time? If so, your reasons for your alternative time slot.

VICKI CONRAN

I wouldn't like to change my time for any other. The last seventy years have seen incredible changes, both political and technological, and to have witnessed and been part of these upheavals has been both exciting and fascinating. I'm sure the world is a much better place today for many more people than it was when I was born in 1931.

CHRONOLOGY

1931 Born 4 October, Esher, Surrey
1945–8 Attends Bryanston School, Dorset
1948–50 Studies at Central School of Arts and Crafts, London
1950–1 Employed by Denis Lennon; works on Festival of Britain
1951 Launches furniture-making business, Conran & Co
1953 Opens the first Soup Kitchen, Chandos Place, London
1954 Opens The Orrery restaurant, King's Road, London
1956 Founds Conran Design Group (CDG)
1962 Moves furniture business to a factory in Thetford, Norfolk
1964 Opens the first Habitat in Fulham Road, London
1968 Merges Habitat with Ryman's to become Ryman Conran
1970 Demerges Habitat from Ryman Conran; sets up Conran Associates
1971 Opens The Neal Street Restaurant, Covent Garden
1973 Opens Habitat in Paris and The Conran Shop in London
1976 Sets up design group at Barton Court
1977 Opens Conran's in New York
1980 Habitat group comprises 47 stores in UK, USA, France and Belgium; founds Conran Roche, architects and town planners
1981 Takes Habitat public; takes over Mothercare; launches Boilerhouse at the V & A after the Conran Foundation established
1983 Habitat–Mothercare acquires Heal's and Richard Shops; start of Butlers Wharf project and Conran Octopus publishers
1985 Sets up Benchmark Woodworking with Sean Sutcliffe
1986 Habitat–Mothercare merges with British Home Stores to create Storehouse plc
1987 Renovation of Michelin Building completed; opens Bibendum and moves The Conran Shop into Michelin Building
1989 Opens the Design Museum and Blue Print Café
1990 Retires as chairman of Storehouse; buys back The Conran Shop
1991 Opens Le Pont de la Tour in Butlers Wharf, London
1992 Opens Cantina del Ponte; opens The Conran Shop in Paris
1993 Opens Quaglino's and Butlers Wharf Chop House
1994 Opens The Conran Shop in Tokyo
1995 Opens Mezzo in Soho, London
1996 Opens The Conran Shop in Hamburg
1997 Opens Bluebird restaurant, bar, club and shop; Zinc Bar & Grill; Orrery restaurant and The Conran Shop, Marylebone
1998 Opens Sartoria and Coq d'Argent restaurants in London; opens Alcazar restaurant in Paris; opens The Conran Shop in Conduit Street, London
1999 Opens second Conran Shop in Paris; launches Conran & Partners
2000 Opens Bridgemarket development in Manhattan with shop and Guastavino's restaurant; opens Great Eastern Hotel, Liverpool Street, London
2001 Sets up new office at Barton Court, Berkshire

CONTRIBUTORS

ABBOTT, Jamie Communications manager for Conran Holdings; Vespa rider.
ARCHER, Jeffrey (Lord Archer of Weston-Super-Mare) Novelist, politician and friend of Andy Colquhoun, who used to work for our design group many years ago.
ARNODIN, Maïmé *Grande dame* of French culture and close friend of Denise Fayolle, for whom I worked on the Prisunic project.
BAKER, Bill Huge wine merchant with a huge appetite for life; consultant to Conran Restaurants.
BARROW, Jean My mother's first cousin; always known as Aunt Jean.
BAVOILLOT, Ghislaine Editor of illustrated books at Flammarion in Paris and French publisher of several of my books.
BAYLEY, Stephen Need I say more?
BIRT, John (Lord Birt) Former director-general of the BBC, a friend.
BLACKMAN, Steven Former communications director for Conran Holdings, now at Deepend.com, a digital communications consultancy that has recently relaunched Conran.com.
BLANC, Raymond Three-star chef of Le Manoir aux Quat'Saisons.
BLAND, Sir Christopher Until recently chairman of the BBC, now of BT; was a non-executive director of Storehouse.
BLOND, Peter Friend; a racing driver, in charge of classic car sales at Sotheby's.
BLOOMBERG, Michael Media mogul and friend.
BODKER, Christopher Restaurateur, competitor and friend of Vicki's (and even of mine).
BODOANO, Bridget Ex-press officer of The Conran Shop, overseeing my 'Plain, Simple and Useful' project.
BOND, Mark Studio head of products and graphics at Conran & Partners.
BRAVO, Rose Marie American chief executive of Burberry, widely credited with restarting the brand.
BULL, Nicholas Managing director of corporate finance at Société Générale; director of the Conran Foundation.
BULLEN, Werner Works for Partners in Marketing, a Belgium-based business that was the first company to throw a party in the private dining room at Mezzo. Submitted his questions via Conran.com.
BURROWS, Cliff Former managing director of Habitat, now at Starbucks.
CAMPBELL, Susan Old friend, illustrator and cookery writer; co-wrote *Poor Cook* with my ex-wife Caroline.
CARLUCCIO, Antonio Brother-in-law, fungophile, TV foodie and owner of The Neal Street Restaurant and Carluccio's Caffès in London.

CHALONER, David Ex-Conran designer, now at Conran Design Group (with which, curiously, I have no connection these days).

CHASE, Simon Marketing director of Hunters & Frankau, cigar merchants.

CHIDSEY, Jonathan Head gardener at Barton Court, cyclist and ex-punk.

CLIFF, Stafford Ex-Conran designer and art director of *The House Book*. Now involved in design journalism, and co-author of the hugely successful 'Style' series for Thames & Hudson.

CONRAN, Ned My youngest son; a father and artist.

CONRAN, Sebastian My eldest son; a father and product designer.

CONRAN, Shirley Superwoman.

CONRAN, Sophie My daughter; a mother, works with Jasper.

CONRAN, Tom My third son; a father, owner of The Cow pub and restaurant and Tom's deli in Notting Hill, London.

CONRAN, Vicki (Lady Conran) Beloved wife. Collaborated with me on my restaurant book.

CRAWFORD, Ilse Ex-editor of *Elle Decoration*, of which I was a contributing editor; later ran Donna Karan's interiors division in New York; most recently founding editor of *Bare*.

CUTLER, Philip An old friend in America, ex-buyer of Macy's and Lord & Taylor. Knows everything that is going on everywhere.

DAVIES, George Former managing director of Next, saviour (we hope) of M & S.

DAVIS, Sir Peter Group chief executive of Sainsbury's, ex-chief executive of the Prudential and Reed Elsevier. I tried to recruit him to run Storehouse.

DAVY, Geoff Ex-managing director of Habitat and BhS.

DEMETRIOS, Eames Grandson of Charles Eames.

DIXSON, Reg My front-seat driver.

DOHERTY, Maureen Ex-muse of Issey Miyake and proprietor of Egg Trading.

DOONE, Richard Architect and managing director of Conran & Partners.

DOWNES, Dr Margaret High-powered Irish businesswoman; ex-partner of Coopers and Lybrand and the first ever female director of the Bank of Ireland; was a non-executive director of Storehouse.

DYSON, James, CBE Designer, entrepreneur, innovator and hero; chairman of trustees of the Design Museum.

ELLIS, Tina A designer with whom I've worked for more years than we care to remember.

EVERAGE, Dame Edna Australian Superwoman.

FARRELL, Sir Terry Award-winning London-based architect and urban designer.

FORD, Anna Broadcaster and friend.

FORD, Tom Creative director of Gucci and YSL.

FORT, Matthew A critic (personal and food).

FORTE, Hon. Sir Rocco Hotelier whose new company, RF Hotels, is establishing an impressive portfolio of idiosyncratically luxurious places to stay.

FOSTER, Norman (Lord Foster of Thames Bank) One of the world's great architects and a great friend.

FRAYLING, Professor Sir Christopher Rector of the Royal College of Art, chairman of the Design Council, trustee of the Design Museum, and deeply knowledgeable film buff.

FRENCH, Nigel Retailing guru.

GALLAGHER, Hattie My stepdaughter. (Does she love me?)

GLYNN SMITH, Georgia Photographer and friend. Her mother Juliet worked on early graphic designs for Habitat.

GRADE, Michael, CBE Impresario; former Channel 4 chief executive and BBC TV director of programmes; chairman of Pinewood Studios.

GRAY, Muriel Glaswegian broadcaster and horror writer. I once appeared in one of her TV programmes and we seemed to get on quite well.

GROSSMAN, Loyd Was paid a substantial advance to write my biography, a project that was subsequently taken over by Nicholas Ind. I once took a guest turn on *Masterchef*.

GUÉRARD, Michel One of France's most distinguished three-star chefs and proprietor with his wife Christine of Les Prés d'Eugénie.

GUNEWARDENA, Des Chief executive of Conran Holdings and a great friend.

HAMBRO, Rupert Financier; chairman of the governors of the Museum of London, which we are redesigning in part.

HAYES, Michael My (personal) lawyer, a partner at Macfarlanes.

HEADING, Jeff Runs the Fulham Road branch of The Conran Shop and has done for many years. One of the nicest men I know.

HEANEY, Maggie Ex-buyer at The Conran Shop. One of the funniest women I know.

HEATHERWICK, Thomas One of the UK's most talented young design polymaths; designer of my gazebo at Barton Court and the curvy art wall installation at Guastavino's in New York.

HEGARTY, John Chairman of Bartle Bogle Hegarty and one of the greatest creative talents in the advertising industry; a trustee of the Design Museum.

HEMPEL, Anouska (Lady Weinberg) Talented designer, hotelier and couturier, married to one of the most long-suffering men I've ever met.

HESELTINE, Michael (Lord Heseltine) Publisher, politician and arboriculturist. We've designed his Haymarket Publishing offices for many years.

HOGG, Min Inspired founding editor of *World of Interiors*, my star student at the Central School, and funny friend.

HOWLAND JACKSON, Wendy Founder of Trams plc, a London-based computer reseller; a great believer in the power of business to help the disadvantaged. Submitted her question via Conran.com.

HUMPHRIES, Barry Shares a bed with Dame Edna and Sir Les.

IND, Nicholas Design journalist and my biographer; now a branding consultant with FutureBrand in Stockholm.

INGRAM, Ann Works in higher education in the north of England and has a particular interest in the work of William Morris.

ISAACSON, Laurence, CBE Operatic restaurateur and my partner at The Creative Business, an advertising company we founded with David Bernstein in the early 1970s.

JOLLANT KNEEBONE, Françoise Ex-design director of the Pompidou Centre, director of ENSCI (Ecole nationale supérieure de création industrielle) and trustee of the Design Museum.

JONES, Wendy My ex-secretary and administrative director of Benchmark.

KAMPRAD, Ingvar Founder of Ikea and current proprietor of Habitat.

KASMIN (John) Art dealer who has represented Hockney and Hodgkin among many others, and great friend. Involved in starting The Neal Street Restaurant and the Garage Gallery.

KEEN, Charles Ex-managing director of Vitra, now chief executive of contract furniture company The Keen Group, of which I'm a small shareholder.

KINSMAN, Rodney Runs OMK Design, a contract furniture company specializing in public seating. He and his wife Lisa are long-time friends.

KIRKPATRICK, Janice Co-founder of Glasgow consultancy Graven Images, this extraordinarily energetic graphic designer lectures, writes and rides motorbikes.

KÖNIGK, Raymund A South Africa-based designer. Submitted his question via Conran.com.

KRANTZ, David Founder of Blazer menswear, which we bought in Storehouse days, now chief executive of Space NK; has remained a friend.

LANG, Jack Ex-French Minister of Culture, currently Minister of Education. Made me a Commander of the Order of Arts and Letters in 1991.

LEE, Jeremy Chef of Blue Print Café and prolific recipe writer. He talks and sings as well.

LEITH, Prue, OBE Caterer and restaurateur; ex-chairman of the Royal Society of Arts and collector of directorships. One of my most docile friends.

LENNOX-BOYD, Arabella (Lady Lennox-Boyd) One of the UK's most talented landscape designers; created the roof garden at Coq d'Argent.

LEO-ANDRIEU, Grace Hong Kong-born hotelier, proprietor of the Hotels Montalembert and Lancaster in Paris.

LEPERCQ, Patrick Managing director of Michelin UK.

LIBBY, Maurice Ex-display manager of Habitat right at the beginning, and a great friend.

LIKIERMAN, Michael Original managing director of Habitat in France; co-founder of the international GrandVision group that owns Vision Express in the UK.

LITTLE, Tim A distinguished cobbler for whom I designed a pair of shoes made from kangaroo hide.

LIVINGSTONE, Ken Mayor of London and soon-to-be neighbour. I recently had a vision of Ken entering his cocoon on the river as a newt and coming out as a Red Admiral butterfly.

LOEWI, David Managing director of Conran Restaurants. Sensitive to physical inducements, I believe.

LUBAOWSKI, John Polish glass merchant and supplier to Habitat and The Conran Shop.

MacCARTHY, Fiona Writer and friend; author of highly praised biographies of William Morris and Eric Gill. Married to David Mellor, cutler and designer. I bought my building at Shad Thames from them.

MALONE, Jo Inspired perfumer. Always smells nice.

MARSHALL, Geoff Ex-managing director of The Conran Shop; one of the most garrulous men I know, but amusing with it.

MAVITY, Roger Used to do the advertising for Habitat, nowadays chief executive of Box Clever.

McINTYRE, Richard Food writer and managing director of a specialist restaurant marketing agency, Carrots & Capers. Submitted his question via Conran.com.

MEADES, Jonathan Crude restaurant critic from the Murdoch manger.

MOIR, Lance Ex-head of corporate finance and planning at Storehouse; now senior lecturer at Cranfield School of Management.

MOONEY (Mounir Houmou-Bedfont) A graphic designer from west London. Submitted his question via Conran.com.

MOWLAM, Marjorie 'Mo' Personal friend and perhaps the bravest and most honest politician I've ever met.

NEWMAN, Sam My fantastic country PA.

The OATES family, including Rebecca and Daphne. Rebecca works as my design assistant at Barton Court.

OSZKO, Zoltan Used to work for Habitat procuring wooden products in Eastern Europe; now works for The Conran Shop in a similar capacity.

PALUMBO, Peter (Lord Palumbo) Ex-chairman of the Arts Council and developer of No. 1 Poultry, the site of Coq d'Argent; a great friend.

PATTERSON, Sir Les Australian cultural attaché and bon viveur.

PEARSON, Dan Garden designer with whom I collaborated on *The Essential Garden Book*.

PEYTON, Oliver Irish restaurateur who's given us the Atlantic Bar & Grill and several dollops of Mash.

PIANIM, Elkin Entrepreneurial forester.

PROUD, Caroline Managing director of Conran Octopus.

PRYKE, Paula Florist with whom we've worked on many of our restaurants.

PYOTT, James Extremely talented graphic designer who used to work for Conran Design and now has his own business.

QUANT, Mary, OBE The fashion symbol of the 1950s and one of the catalysts of the 'Swinging Sixties'. I was a school friend of her late husband Alexander Plunket Greene and designed her Knightsbridge branch of Bazaar.

QUEENSBERRY, David (twelfth Marquess of) A great friend who brought Shirley into my life. Always plays by the rules. Ex-professor of ceramics at the Royal College; like me, designed for Midwinter in the 1950s.

RADICE, Vittorio Ex-managing director of Habitat, now reviving Selfridges.

RAWSTHORN, Alice The brilliant new director of the Design Museum; another ex-punk.

RETTIE, Nicholas Managing director of the Great Eastern Hotel, recently Hotelier of the Year.

RICHARDSON, Julie Ex-PR and marketing manager for Conran Restaurants.

RITBLAT, John Property developer; chairman of The British Land Company.

ROBINSON, Amanda My fantastic urban PA.

ROBINSON, Nick Ex-Habitat furniture buyer, now joint managing director of The Conran Shops (with Michel Cultru).

RONAY, Egon Publisher of eponymous guides that have helped promulgate the British food revolution.

ROSE, John Director of humanities at my alma mater, Bryanston.

ROWAN, Peter A graphic designer who as a student was inspired by the Boilerhouse project. Submitted his question via Conran.com.

SAINSBURY, John (Lord Sainsbury of Preston Candover) Friend and one-time colleague on the board of Savacentre.

SALZ, Anthony Senior partner of Freshfields; acted for Storehouse on a number of deals during the 1980s.

SEELIG, Roger Ex-director of Morgan Grenfell; took Habitat public, acquired Mothercare for us and acted on many other deals.

SEROTA, Sir Nicholas Revolutionary director of Tate; the energy behind Tate Modern.

SIMMS, Paul Student at the University of Nottingham; recently worked for a short time as an adviser for the relaunch of Conran.com, through which he submitted his questions.

SMITH, Alan K P Ex-director of Marks & Spencer, then at Woolworths, then chairman of Storehouse, now chairman of Mothercare. When he was at M & S I tried to poach him to run Storehouse.

SMITH, Diane and Ian Housekeepers at Barton Court, keeping it running like well-oiled machinery.

SMITH, Richard An artist living in New York and a long-time friend, whose work I have commissioned and collected.

SOANE, James An ex-director of Conran & Partners; worked with me on the Great Eastern Hotel and Guastavino's.

SORRELL, John Originally of Newell & Sorrell graphic designers; ex-chairman of the Design Council; friend.

STEINER, Rupert Financial journalist on the *Sunday Times*; seems to follow our activities quite closely.

STODDART, Michael An ex-director of Hepworth's and Next; chairman of a financial company called Electra. I served as a board member on its subsidiary Electra Risk Capital.

SUDJIC, Deyan Design and architecture writer; one of the founders of *Blueprint* magazine, now editor of *Domus*. Great friend.

SUMMERS, Andrew Chief executive of the Design Council.

SUTCLIFFE, Sean Runs Benchmark. One of my best friends; my children refer to him as my fifth son.

SWENGLEY, Nicole Freelance journalist; regularly writes for the *Evening Standard*.

TANG, David, OBE Hong Kong entrepreneur, owner of Shanghai Tang and cigar aficionado. Socialite *par excellence*.

TWEEDY, Colin Chief executive of Arts & Business, a Butlers Wharf-based organization that develops 'creative partnerships' (in other words redistributes wealth) between business and artists.

WEBB, Jill Buying director of The Conran Shops; a keen eye that matches mine.

WHEATCROFT, Patience Business editor of *The Times*; used to edit *Retail Week*. Great sense of humour, very perceptive.

WICKHAM, Julyan My great friend Michael Wickham's son; a talented architect and designer of restaurants, including Bank and Kensington Place in London.

WIGLEY, Bob Worked with Nicholas Bull at Morgan Grenfell; nowadays co-head of investment banking at Merrill Lynch. Romantically attached to Brunelys, which he has visited on a number of occasions.

WILLIAMS, Graham Managing director of Bibendum and friend.

WILLIS, Simon My one-time editor at Conran Octopus, later communications director of Conran Holdings, now at the Great Eastern Hotel. Terrible on Monday mornings.

WOOD, Matthew and ZARA, Paul Architects and directors of Conran & Partners; professionally inseparable.

INDEX

PICTURE CREDITS

The publisher would like to thank the following photographers and organizations, and Terence Conran's friends and family, for their kind permission to reproduce the photographs in this book:

10 courtesy of Priscilla Carluccio; **12** Science Photo Library; **13–17** courtesy of Priscilla Carluccio; **20** courtesy of Terence Conran; **23** courtesy of Priscilla Carluccio; **24** Jerry Harpur; **25** Mike McNamee/Science Photo Library; **26–32** courtesy of Terence Conran; **33** London Weekend TV; **34** courtesy of Bryanston School; **37** courtesy of Terence Conran; Lucia Eames/Eames Office (www.eamesoffice.com); **40** courtesy of Cynthia Manners; **42** Michael Wickham courtesy of Cynthia Manners; **44** Design Council/DHRC; **45** courtesy of Terence Conran; **46** Mary Evans Picture Library; **47** London Metropolitan Archive; **51** Terence Conran Printed Textile Design published by The Studio Ltd **52** Cecil Beaton/Camera Press; **53** above David Montgomery; **53** below Christian Sarramon; **55** Robert Capa/Magnum; **57** courtesy of Anita Story; **59** above & below left Hulton Collection; **59** below right Popperfoto; **63–64** above RIBA Library Photographs Collection; **64** below courtesy of Terence Conran; **65** RIBA Library Photographs Collection; **66** Terence Donovan courtesy of Terence Conran; **69** Paul Almasy/AKG; **72** courtesy of Mary Quant; **73** RIBA Library Photographs Collection; **76** Chris Dawes; **77** RIBA Library Photographs Collection; **78** V & A Picture Library; **80** RIBA Library Photographs Collection; **81–3** V & A Picture Library; **84** above courtesy of Kasmin; **84** below V & A Picture Library; **86** V & A Picture Library; **87** courtesy of Terence Conran; **89** V & A Picture Library; **90** above left & below right Advertising Archive; **90** above right RIBA Library Photographs Collection; **90** below left V & A Picture Library; **92** The Times Newspaper, London; **97** V & A Picture Library; **98–9** courtesy of Terence Conran; **103–4** Peter Cook/View; **111** courtesy of Michelin Tyre plc; **114** London Metropolitan Archives; **115** above courtesy of Terence Conran; **115** below courtesy of Conran & Partners; **118** Georgia Glynn Smith; **121** courtesy of Kasmin; **122** above left Georgia Glynn Smith; **122** above right Ray Main/Mainstream; **122** below Chris Gascoigne/View; **126** courtesy of Conran Restaurants; **128** Chris Grieves/Associated Press; **131** above Jean-François Pin/Katz Pictures; **131** below Georgia Glynn Smith; **132** Peter Cook/View; **136** courtesy of Conran Restaurants; **137** Steve Speller/designer: Thomas Heatherwick; **140** T A Wilkie/Camera Press; **141** above left & below courtesy of Conran Restaurants; **141** above right Marianne Majerus; **143** courtesy of l'Oustau de Baumanière **146** Craig Knowles/Country Life Picture Library; **148–9** RIBA Library Photographs Collection; **151** Bauhaus-Archiv Berlin; **155** Dyson; **154** The Conran Shop; **157** above Ross Harrison Koty/Gettyone Stone; **157** below Jefferson Smith/Design Museum; **159** Ezra Stoller/Esto; **160** above AKG; **160** below The Glasgow Picture Library; **161** Courtesy of Terence Conran; **162** courtesy of Conran Restuarants; **163** Robert Olding/Photonica; **165** O Roques/Rogery/PDV/Camera Press; **170** courtesy of Terence Conran; **175** Design Museum; **176** Design Council Slide Collection at The Manchester Metropolitan University; **178** above courtesy of Conran & Partners; **178** below Jefferson Smith/Design Museum; **179** Poul Ib Henriksen; **184** courtesy of Antonio and Priscilla Carluccio **185** Steve Speller/designer: Thomas Heatherwick; **187** courtesy of Ahrends Burton Koralek Architects; **188** Ezra Stoller/Esto/Arcaid; **189** Peter Cook/View; **192** Dennis Gilbert/View; **197** above Atlantic Syndication; **197** below Andrew Lawson; **207–11** courtesy of Terence Conran; **211** courtesy of Ned Conran; **212** Jerry Harpur; **214** Christopher Hirsheimer; **220** above Iain Sarjeant/Bruce Coleman Collection; **220** below Christian Sarramon; **223** left Verne Fotografie; **223** right Simon Wheeler; **224** Christian Sarramon; **226** Hulton Collection; **228** courtesy of Kasmin; **229** courtesy of Terence Conran; **231** Lorenzo Agius; **232** Theodore Wood/Camera Press; **236** Verne Fotografie; **237** Jerry Harpur; **238** Christian Sarramon; **241** courtesy of Terence Conran; **245** Mark Stewart/Camera Press

Every effort has been made to trace the copyright holders and we apologize in advance for any unintentional omission. We will be pleased to insert the appropriate acknowledgement in any subsequent edition.